chain*style*

50 CONTEMPORARY JEWELRY DESIGNS

JANE DICKERSON

INTERWEAVE.
interweavestore.com

Photography Joe Coca
Photo Stylist Ann Sabine Swanson
Design Karla Baker, Liz Quan
Technical Editor Jamie Hogsett
Production Katherine Jackson

Interweave Press LLC
201 East Fourth Street
Loveland, CO 80537-5655 USA
interweavestore.com

Printed in China by Asia Pacific Offset

Library of Congress Cataloging-in-Publication Data

Dickerson, Jane.
 Chain style : 50 contemporary jewelry designs / Jane Dickerson.
    p. cm.
 Includes bibliographical references and index.
 ISBN 978-1-59668-150-7 (pbk.)
 1. Jewelry making. 2. Metal-work. 3. Chains (Jewelry) 4. Beadwork. I. Title.

TT212.D52 2009
739.27--dc22
2009008798

10 9 8 7 6 5 4 3 2 1

Acknowledgments

My heartfelt thanks to the artists who contributed their time, talent, and unique designs to this book. Your willingness to share the soul of your art is inspiring and motivating. Your generosity makes it possible for others to learn, grow, and follow in your path. Thank you.

Thank you to all of those at Interweave who made this book so beautiful: Steve Koenig, Tricia Waddell, Rebecca Campbell, Jamie Hogsett, Liz Quan, Karla Baker, Katherine Jackson, and Joe Coca.

A very special thanks to Ann and Paul Pillion for all of their love and support. There are no words big enough to express my gratitude.

Thank you to Carol Kowitt and Naushad Jessani for giving me the tools to work with and grow. Your encouragement and constancy have brought me to this place.

A big thank you to my wonderful friends who have inspired me, nudged me, made me laugh, and enticed me to come out and play. Thank you for your friendship.

Bailey and Banks, my two cats, participated in all my designs, sometimes tasting them as well. There is always room for you on my worktable.

Jane Dickerson

Contents

PROJECTS

INTRODUCTION

RESOURCES

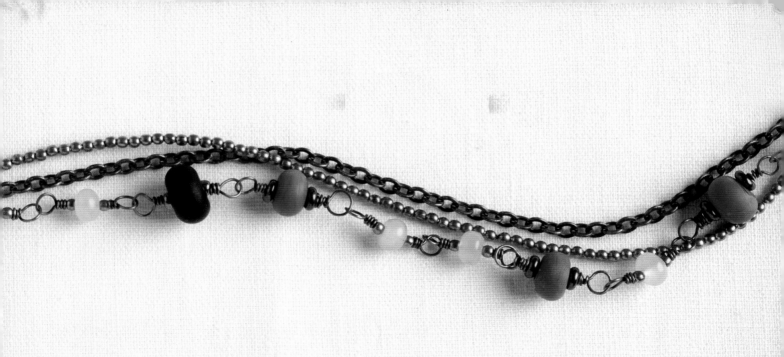

Are you a beginner? New to jewelry making?

This book is the perfect place to start. The great thing about designing with chain is how fast you can create a finished piece. A few special beads connected with random lengths of chain can make a fabulous necklace in minutes! And there are so many types of chain to choose from: cable, curb, rolo, figure-eight, and anchor—to name just a few. Then there are chains I've discovered while writing this book that are too hard to describe because they're so unique.

All of the techniques used in this book are suitable for beginners. The finished designs will offer a range of complexity but all use basic jewelry-making skills. Some of the techniques you'll learn are: opening and closing jump rings, cutting chain, oxidizing silver, hammering materials for texture, creating wire-wrapped loops, and making your own jump rings.

The tools and materials for the projects inside are easy to find. You will have no problem finding an enormous selection of chain to choose from. It's everywhere—bead shows, bead shops, craft stores, and online. I found a store in New York that had a complete wall of chain! You'll find resources included for all of the chain used in this book.

Chain is easy on the budget, too, particularly if you use base metal chain. Stretch your beading materials by incorporating chain in your designs. Don't throw anything away—every link on a chain has the potential of becoming a jump ring, and every scrap of chain can turn into a one-of-a-kind bracelet.

Enjoy the beautiful projects crafted by these wonderful, gifted artists. Let them inspire you to explore all types of chain that appeals to you. Use their designs as a jumping-off point for your own unique style. There's no limit to what you can create, one link at a time!

Jane Dickerson

Chain is defined as a flexible series of joined links. It comes

in every size and shape imaginable from bicycle chain to daisy chain to snow tire chain to dangle-a-diamond-on-a-platinum-cable chain. As long as it's linked together—it's chain.

Whatever your price range, there's a type of chain to complement your jewelry design. If you're on a budget, working with base-metal chain is a great option. Base metal is a nonprecious metal such as steel, aluminum, brass, copper, nickel, pewter, and titanium. You'll find several projects using base metal in this book. Precious-metal chains (gold, silver, and platinum) are more costly—silver being the least expensive. Try mixing a base metal with a precious metal. For example, you could use silver and copper together. Mixing metals not only creates a unique look, it keeps the cost of your piece down.

You can buy chain in bulk, by the foot, or already fashioned into a necklace, bracelet, or earrings. Standard necklace lengths range from 18" to 30" (46 to 76 cm) for men and 16" to 36" (41 to 91 cm) for women. Standard bracelet lengths range from 7" to 7½" (18 to 19 cm) for women and 8½" to 9" (22 to 23 cm) for men. For extra flexibility in length, some types of chain allow for you to hook the clasp at different points on the chain, thereby shortening or lengthening the necklace. You can also add a chain extender to almost any jewelry design by attaching a few extra inches of cable chain and then hooking the clasp to any link on the extender.

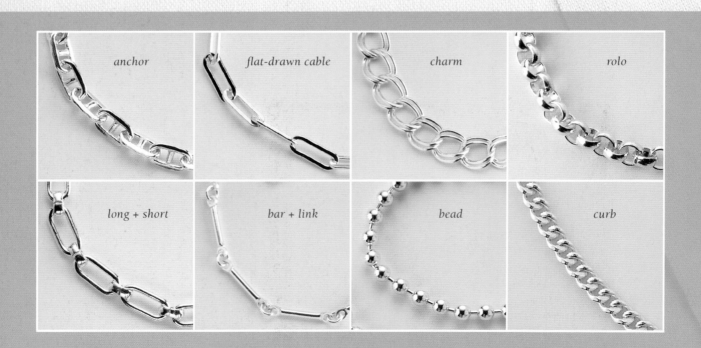

anchor

flat-drawn cable

charm

rolo

long + short

bar + link

bead

curb

Common jewelry-making tools are used for all the chain work in this book. Unfortunately, you'll find that many jewelry-making tool kits sold at craft stores have the wrong kind of pliers, so beware. Make sure the jaws of your pliers have a smooth surface—don't use tools with teeth, like the kind you get from the hardware store. And even the right kind of pliers may need some extra attention. Try dipping them in Tool Magic, a heavy-duty rubber coating, to prevent marring the chain. You can also use adhesive tape in a pinch.

To cut the chain, use heavy-duty flush cutters and make as clean a cut as possible. Flush cut both sides of the link, otherwise you will have a beveled edge on one side and a flat edge on the other, and the link will not close properly. Save any extra links you remove from your chain to use as jump rings in another project. To open and close chain, always use two pairs of chain-nose pliers. Use the same technique as you would use for opening and closing a jump ring. Grasp each side of the link with your pliers and push one side away from you while pulling the other side toward you, so the ring opens from side to side. Reverse the direction to close the link. You never want to pull the chain as this will weaken the link and pull it out of shape.

There is an unlimited variety of chain to choose from. You'll find it at craft stores, bead shops, bead shows, jewelry suppliers, and online. The following samples of chain are provided courtesy of Rio Grande and are for identification purposes only. The chain included in this book comes from multiple suppliers, and the specific type of chain used in a project may be subject to the retailer's individual identification methods.

rope

Boston link

box

cable

figaro

venetian box

figure eight

wheat herringbone

French rope

woven

Tools Most chain jewelry projects require only two tools—pliers and cutters. Of course, if you are planning to make your own jump rings or chain, there are plenty of supplemental tools to help simplify and enhance your work. Most workshops should have a set of good pliers and hammers, an anvil or steel bench block on which to hammer, some metal files for smoothing, and a supply of various-size mandrels around which you can coil wire. Mandrels can be anything from specialty tools for jewelry makers to pens and pencils, or even chopsticks!

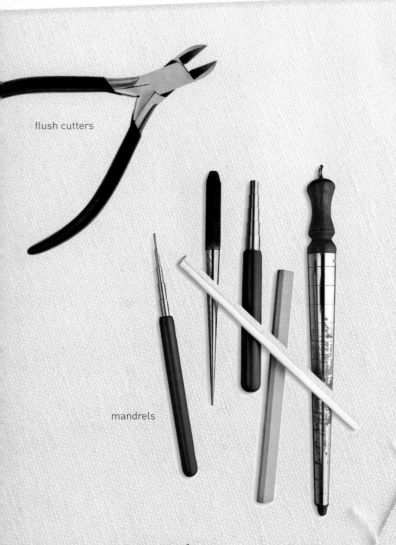

flush cutters

mandrels

GENERAL TOOLS

Flush cutters
These are also called side cutters because the cut is made to the side. They have pointed, angled jaws that allow very close cuts in tight places. One side of the jaws is almost flat, the other concave. Always hold the flat side of the cutters against your work and the concave side against the waste. The flat side provides a nice flush end to your work. Flush cutters should be sold with a maximum gauge-cutting capacity; be sure to use cutters that can accommodate the wire you're using.

Mandrels
A mandrel is a spindle, rod, or bar around which you can bend metal or wire. They come in a variety of shapes and sizes. Some are made specifically for bracelets, some for rings, and some for making bezels. Almost anything can be used as a mandrel to shape wire, including wooden dowels, even other pieces of wire. A Sharpie marker is a good example—it's the perfect shape to make French ear wires.

Wire gauge
Also known as the Brown & Sharpe wire gauge, this tool looks a bit like a flat round gear. It measures the diameter of your wire and is an essential tool for wire jewelry making.

wire gauge

chain-nose

PLIERS

Bent-nose pliers

Also called bent chain-nose, these are similar to chain-nose pliers but have a bend at the tip that allows access to tight places for tasks like tightening coils and tucking in ends. Two pairs used together are also useful for opening and closing jump rings.

Chain-nose pliers

The workhorse of wire tools, chain-nose pliers are like needle-nose pliers but without teeth that can mar your wire. They are used for grasping wire, opening and closing jump rings, and making sharp angled bends. They get their name from chain makers, and it's a good idea to have at least two pairs in your workshop.

Flat-nose pliers

Flat-nose pliers have broad, flat jaws and are good for making sharp bends in wire, grasping spirals, and holding components.

Round-nose pliers

Another wireworker's necessity, round-nose pliers have pointed, graduated round jaws. They are used for making jump rings, simple loops, and curved bends in wire.

Wire-straightening pliers

These are also called nylon-jaw pliers because the jaws are made of hard nylon. Pulling wire through the clamped jaws will straighten any bends or kinks. They can also be used to hold, bend, or shape wire without marring the metal. Keep in mind that every time you pull wire through straightening pliers, you're hardening it more, making it more brittle and harder to work with.

flat-nose

wire-straightening

round-nose

bent-nose

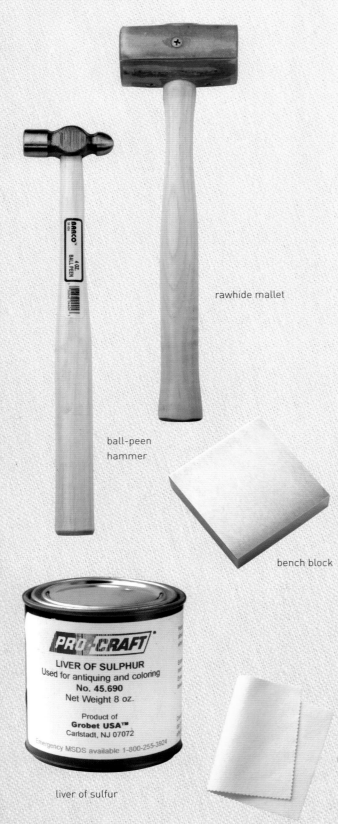

rawhide mallet

ball-peen
hammer

bench block

liver of sulfur

polishing cloth

HAMMERING TOOLS

Ball-peen hammer

Another staple in the studio, this hammer has one round half-domed head and one round flat head. The half-domed head is used for making little dents for texture, while the flat head is used for flattening wire.

Rawhide mallet

A hammer made of hide, this can be used on metal and wire without marring it. They're good for tapping wire into place or for hardening wire.

Steel bench block

A bench block provides a small and portable hard surface on which to hammer wire. They're made of polished steel and are usually only ¼" (2 cm) thick and a few inches square. Use a bench block with a ball-peen hammer for flattening or texturing wire.

FINISHING TOOLS

Liver of sulfur

Liver of sulfur is a chemical traditionally used to darken silver. It comes in a liquid or solid chunk form and is used in oxidizing or antiquing silver and copper. When a small amount is mixed with hot water, it will turn a piece that is dipped in it from blue to gray to black. This transition happens quickly, so you'll want to keep an eye on it.

Polishing cloth

Jewelry polishing cloths are infused with a polishing compound and can be used for cleaning metal, eliminating tarnish, and hardening wire—pulling wire through the cloth repeatedly will stiffen it.

Techniques

Similar to tools, there are a few basic techniques required to make jewelry with chain. If you can open and close jump rings and learn to make a nice round loop with your round-nose pliers, you're halfway there! Polishing and oxidizing can also add a nice finishing touch.

The secret to pretty chain jewelry is neatness. Chain links and jump rings should be closed precisely, and wire-wrapped ends should be neat and smooth or tucked out of sight. Coils should be tight and uniform (or free-form if that's what you're going for), and loops should be round and centered.

BASICS

Using a wire gauge
Brown & Sharpe or AWG (American Wire Gauge) is the standard in the United States for measuring the diameter of wire. When you use a wire gauge, use the small slots around the edge of the gauge, not the round holes at the ends of the slots. Place the wire edge into a slot into which it fits. If there's wiggle room, place it into the next smaller slot. When you reach a slot into which it will not fit, then the number at the end of the next larger slot is the gauge of your wire.

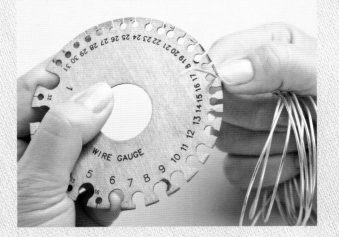

Flush cutting
Flush cutters have two sides, a flat side and a concave side. When you cut wire, you want the end that remains on your working piece to be flat, or flush. To do this, make sure the flat side of the cutters is facing your working piece when you snip.

Straightening wire
Pulling a piece of wire through nylon-jaw pliers will straighten any bends in the wire. Grasp one end of the wire tightly in the nylon jaws and pull with your other hand. It may take two or three pulls through the pliers to straighten the wire completely. Be aware that the manipulation of wire in any pliers, including nylon-jaw pliers, will start the process of work-hardening the wire, which will eventually make it stiffer and harder to work with.

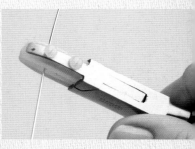

Hammering
Always grasp the hammer firmly near the end of the handle. Do not "choke up" on the handle as you might a baseball bat. This assures you're using the weight of the head optimally and also keeps your hand from absorbing the shock of the impact.

LOOPS

Simple loops

Grasp the end of the wire in round-nose pliers so you can just see the tip of the wire (1). Rotate the pliers fully until you've made a complete loop (2). Remove the pliers. Reinsert the tip of the pliers to grasp the wire directly across from the opening of the loop (3). Make a sharp 45° bend across from the opening, centering the loop over the length of the wire like a lollipop (4).

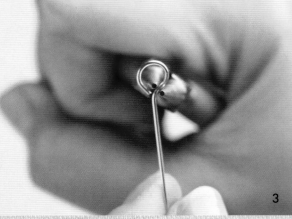

1

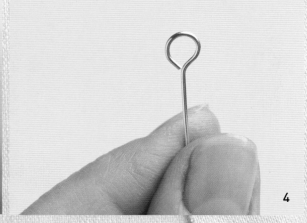

2

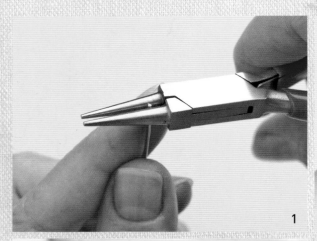

3

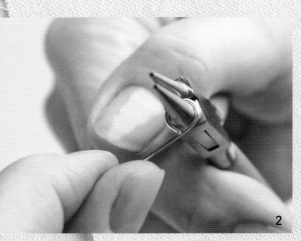

4

Wrapped loops

Grasp the wire about 2" (5 cm) from the end with chain-nose pliers. Using your fingers, bend the wire flat against the pliers to 90° **(1)**. With round-nose pliers, grasp the wire right at the bend you just made, holding the pliers perpendicular to the tabletop. Pull the wire up and over the top of the round-nose pliers **(2)**. Pull the pliers out and put the lower jaw back into the loop you just made **(3)**. Continue pulling the wire around the bottom jaw of the pliers into a full round loop **(4)**. With your fingers or chain-nose pliers, wrap the wire around the neck of the lower wire two or three times **(5)**. Trim the excess wrapped wire **(6)**.

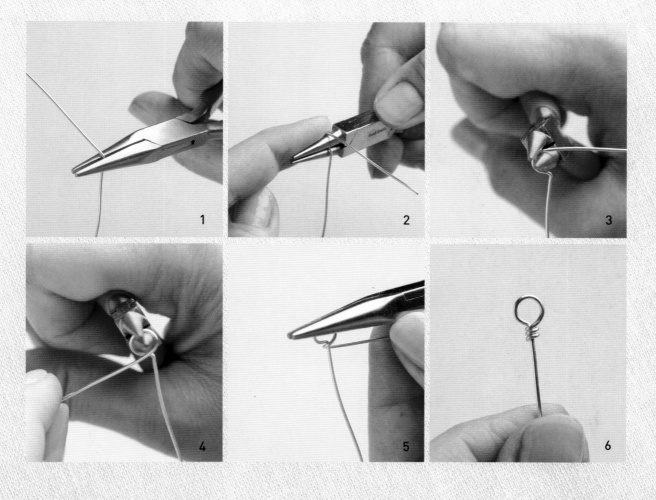

Briolette loops

For top-drilled stones, insert a wire through the hole and bend up both sides so that they cross over the top of the stone **(1)**. (You will only need a short length on one side.) Make a bend in each of the wires so they point straight up off the top of the stone. With flush cutters, trim the short wire so that it's no longer than ⅛" (3 mm) long **(2)**. Pinch the two wires together with chain-nose pliers and bend the longer wire over the top of the shorter wire to 90° **(3)**. Make a wrapped loop by switching to round-nose pliers and pulling the long wire up and over the round jaw **(4–5)**. Wrap the neck of the two wires together two or three times to secure **(6)**. Trim the excess wrapped wire **(7)**.

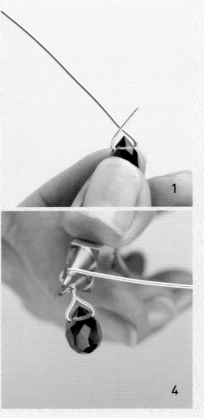

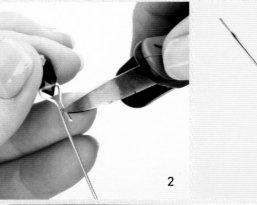

COILS AND SPIRALS

Coiling

Coiling can be done on any round mandrel, including another piece of wire. Hold one end of the wire tightly against the mandrel with your thumb and coil the length up the mandrel (1). Be sure to wrap snugly and keep the coils right next to one another. Flush cut both ends of the coiled wire (2). Slide the coil off the mandrel.

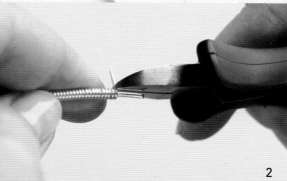

Spiraling

Make a very small loop with round-nose pliers (1). Grasp the loop in flat-nose pliers and use the thumb of your other hand to push the wire around the loop (2). Continue to move the spiral around in the jaws of the flat-nose pliers to enable you to enlarge the coil (3).

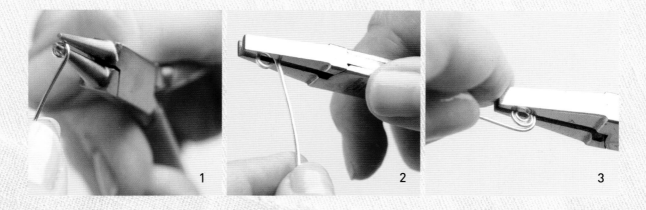

JUMP RINGS

Making jump rings

Coil the wire snugly around a mandrel (1). Each single coil will make one jump ring. Remove the mandrel. Using flush cutters, cut through all the rings at the same spot along the length of the coil, snipping one or two at a time (2). They will fall away and each ring will be slightly open (3). Flush cut the beveled side of each jump ring so both sides are flush cut and the jump ring will close properly.

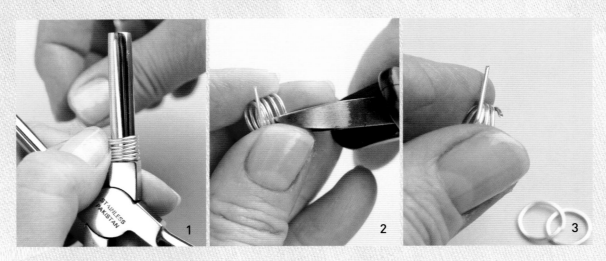

Opening and closing jump rings

Always use two pairs of chain-nose or bent-nose pliers to open and close jump rings. Grasp the ring on each side of the opening with pliers (1). Gently push one side away from you while pulling the other side toward you, so the ring opens from side to side (2). To close, reverse the directions of your hands.

Note

When purchasing jump rings, note that some vendors sell them by inner diameter measurements, and some vendors sell them by outer diameter measurements. The difference is miniscule and only important if you're working on a complex chain mail design.

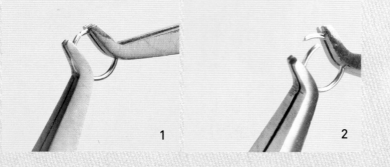

LINKS

Figure-eight links

Using round-nose pliers, make a loop on one end of the wire (1). Remove the pliers and grasp the wire just below the loop you just made. Pull the wire around the jaw of the pliers in the opposite direction of the first loop (2). Make sure you work at the same point on the jaw that you made the first loop so that the loops are the same size. Flush cut the end. Hold one loop with your fingers, grasp the other loop with chain-nose pliers, and twist a quarter turn so that the loops sit perpendicular to each other (3).

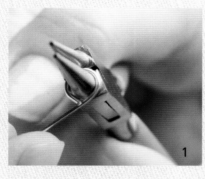
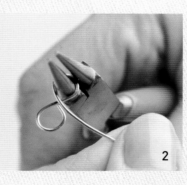
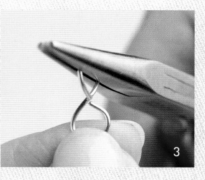

HOOKS

Simple hooks

Make a simple loop on the end of the wire. Hold a Sharpie marker against the wire above the loop and bend the wire over the marker and down parallel to the loop (1). Flush cut the long wire across from the loop. With round-nose pliers, make a small bend outward at the end of the hook (2–3). Flatten the curve of the hook with a ball-peen hammer to work-harden and strengthen the hook (4).

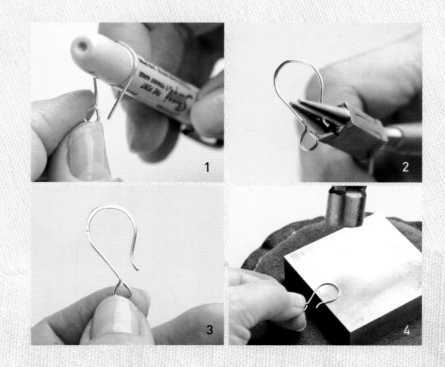

Spiral hooks

This clasp can be made with a tight spiral or a loose, open spiral. Both begin with a small loop made with round-nose pliers **(1)**. With flat-nose or nylon-jaw pliers, make your spiral **(2)**. Leave about 2" (5 cm) beyond the spiral, and at the other end of the wire flatten ¼" (6 mm) with a ball-peen hammer **(3)**. Make a very small loop in the opposite direction as the spiral **(4)**. Using either pliers or a mandrel such as a Sharpie pen, bend the length back away from the small loop and into a hook **(5)**. Flatten the curve of the hook with a ball-peen hammer to work-harden and strengthen the hook **(6–7)**.

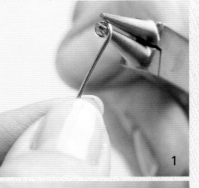

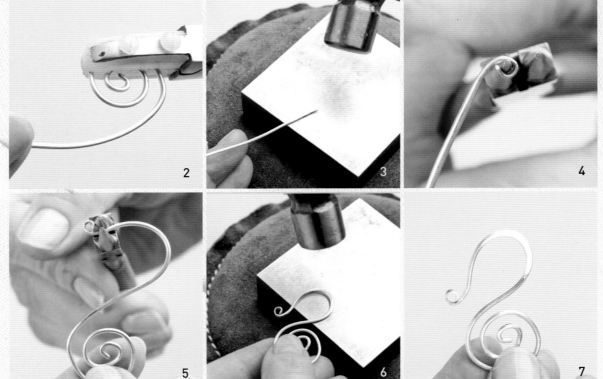

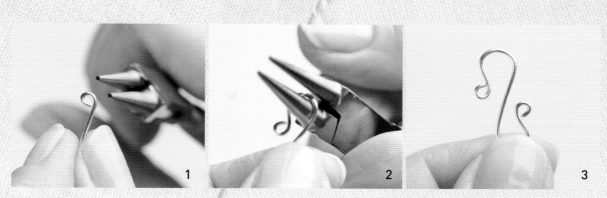

S-hooks

This clasp can be made in any size, depending upon the length of wire you start with. Using round-nose pliers, make a small loop on each end, going in opposite directions (1). Grasp one end with the base of the round-nose pliers just below the loop, and with the loop facing you. Turn the pliers away from you, rolling the wire completely over, forming a hook (2). Repeat on the other end (3).

OTHER TECHNIQUES

Oxidizing

Liver of sulfur is used to darken, or patina, silver and copper. Dissolve a small lump of liver of sulfur in very hot water. Dip your piece into the solution (1–2). Depending upon the temperature of the solution and the length of time you leave the piece in it, the metal can turn a variety of colors, including gold, blue, and black. Remove the piece (3). Rinse, dry, and polish lightly to remove some of the patina and leave the darkened color in the recesses of the piece (4–5).

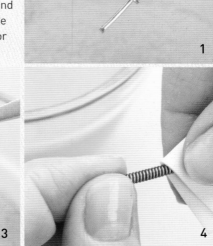

Projects

The great thing about designing with chain is how quickly you can make a finished piece of jewelry. Some of the projects only take a few minutes to make, and they look fabulous! Others are more complex but still just use basic jewelry-making techniques. I love all of them and hope you do, too!

spice
Taya and Silvija Koschnick

With just a hint of the exotic, this bracelet is a contemporary take on ethnic jewelry, blending traditional Afghani serpentine jade with beautifully faceted peridot and brown garnets.

MATERIALS

3 links of sterling silver 13×20mm flattened cable chain

4½" (11 cm) of sterling silver 6×8mm flattened cable chain

8 grossular (green and brown) garnet 4mm rondelles

7 Afghan jade 4mm rondelles

4 peridot 4mm rondelles

1 Afghan jade 5×8mm oval

18 sterling silver 26-gauge 2" (5 cm) head pins

1 sterling silver 24-gauge 3" (8 cm) head pin

2 sterling silver 6mm jump rings

1 sterling silver 5mm jump ring

1 sterling silver 4mm jump ring

1 sterling silver 11mm lobster clasp

TOOLS

2 pairs of chain-nose pliers

Flush cutters

Liver of sulfur

0000 extra-fine steel wool

Finished size: 7½" (19 cm)

All materials: Bead Paradise.

1 Clean and oxidize all the sterling silver (see page 21 for instructions). Use the steel wool to gently remove the excess patina until you reach your desired shade. Cut the small chain into one 2¾" (7 cm) piece and one 1¾" (4.5 cm) piece (one piece should be 3 links longer than the other).

2 Use one 26-gauge head pin to string one 4mm rondelle. Form a wrapped loop that attaches to one of the 3 links of the large cable chain. Repeat entire step, attaching a total of 5 dangles each to the two side links and 7 dangles to the center link.

3 Use one 6mm jump ring to attach the end of the longer piece of chain cut in Step 1 to one end link of the large chain. Repeat this step to attach the shorter piece of chain to the other end link of the large chain. Use one 26-gauge head pin to string 1 rondelle; form a wrapped loop that attaches to one 6mm jump ring. Repeat to attach 1 dangle to the other jump ring.

4 Use the 5mm jump ring to attach the other end of the 1¾" (4.5 cm) cable chain to the lobster clasp. Use the 24-gauge head pin to string the jade oval; form a wrapped loop. Use the 4mm jump ring to attach the wrapped loop to the other end of the 2¾" (7 cm) chain.

live out loud

Yvonne Irvin

The combination of materials in this necklace really makes it come to life. With vibrant aluminum jump rings, colorful enamel and metallic chains, and beautiful one-of-a-kind handpainted Plexiglas components, this necklace shouts "fun" through and through.

MATERIALS

22" (56 cm) of blue 5.5×4mm metallic cable chain

22" (56 cm) of turquoise 5.5×4mm metallic cable chain

22" (56 cm) of purple 5.5×4mm baked enamel cable chain

MyElements components:

3 acrylic 18mm circles

4 acrylic 8mm circles

3 acrylic 12mm circles

1 acrylic 15mm donut

3 acrylic 10×20mm ovals

Anodized aluminum jump rings:

3 size 22mm 10-gauge: 1 turquoise, 2 purple

3 size 13mm 14-gauge: 2 turquoise, 1 purple

11 size 9mm 16-gauge: 5 purple, 6 turquoise

54 size 6mm 20-gauge: purple

1 sterling silver 40×11mm Live Out Loud connector

1 sterling silver 15mm 8-hole rotary link

1 hand-enameled 35mm washer

4 purple 7mm vinyl rings

2 blue 7mm vinyl rings

11 assorted 6mm Greek ceramic gears

7 assorted lampworked glass beads and charms

3 size 6mm glass donuts

1 size 10mm glass donut

23 assorted 2–8mm glass and silver beads

10 silver 2" (5 cm) head pins

6" (15 cm) of purple 20-gauge colored copper wire

1 purple 20mm hook-and-eye clasp

TOOLS

Round-nose pliers

2 pairs of chain-nose pliers

Flush cutters

Dremel tool or hand drill

$1/16$" drill bit

Finished size: 29" (74 cm)

Lampworked beads: Laura Drosner Schreiber, Deepwood Art, Braker Beads, and Keoki Art Glass. Live Out Loud connector: Hip Chicks Beads. MyElements components and all other findings: MyElements, Yvonne Irvin.

1   Use 3" (8 cm) of purple wire to form a wrapped loop
    that attaches to 1 lampworked glass charm. String
    1 assorted glass bead and form a wrapped loop. Set
    aside the glass charm link. Use the remaining purple
    wire to form a wrapped loop. String 1 assorted glass
    bead, 1 blue vinyl ring, the largest of the lampworked
    glass beads, 1 purple vinyl ring, and 1 blue vinyl ring;
    form a wrapped loop. Set aside the lampworked glass
    bead link. Use 1 head pin to string 1 lampworked glass
    bead; form a wrapped loop. Repeat twice for a total of 3
    lampworked glass dangles. Mix the remaining assorted
    beads. Use 1 head pin to string 2 or 3 beads and form a
    wrapped loop. Repeat six times for a total of 7 assorted
    glass dangles. Set aside.

2   Cut 3" (8 cm) of each color chain. Starting at the bottom
    of the necklace, attach the chain to both sides of the
    Live Out Loud connector using one 9mm purple jump

ring on one side and one 9mm turquoise jump ring on
the other side. Use one 6mm jump ring to attach the
glass charm link to the purple jump ring.

3   Use 6mm jump rings to attach the following MyEle-
    ments components to the turquoise chain on the left:
    all the 8mm circles, two 12mm circles, and all the
    ovals. Use 6mm jump rings to attach 5 Greek ceramic
    gears to the purple chain on the right side. Use one
    22mm purple jump ring to attach the focal washer to
    the center of all 3 pieces of chain.

4   Cut 12" (30.5 cm) from each color chain. Attach one
    9mm turquoise jump ring to one end of each chain. Use
    one 9mm turquoise jump ring to attach the previous
    9mm turquoise jump ring to the 9mm turquoise jump
    ring used in Step 2. Use one 13mm purple jump ring to
    attach 1 lampworked glass charm to the 9mm tur-

quoise jump ring attached to the chains. Use one 6mm jump ring to attach one 12mm MyElements circle to the middle turquoise jump ring.

5 Use two 6mm jump rings to attach 1 lampworked glass dangle to two 6mm jump rings. Open one 22mm purple jump ring and string 5 ceramic gears and the two 6mm jump rings just used; close the jump ring. Use two 6mm jump rings to attach the 22mm jump ring to the right side of the Live Out Loud connector. Attach two 13mm turquoise jump rings to the 22mm jump ring.

6 Attach one 6mm jump ring to one side of 1 MyElements 18mm circle and attach one 9mm turquoise jump ring to the other side. Use two 6mm jump rings to attach 1 lampworked glass dangle and the 6mm jump ring side of the circle to the two 13mm turquoise jump rings from Step 4. Use two 6mm jump rings to connect one side of the stacked lampworked glass bead link to the 9mm turquoise jump ring on the 18mm circle. Use one 9mm turquoise jump ring to attach 1 assorted glass dangle to the 9mm turquoise jump ring. Use one 6mm jump ring to attach 1 lampworked glass dangle to the first loop of the lampworked glass bead link. Use the 22mm turquoise jump ring to string 3 purple vinyl rings and the other side of the lampworked glass bead link.

7 Drill 3 new holes in each remaining 18mm circle ⅛" (3.2 mm) in from the edge. For the left circle: one at 1:00, to the right of the existing top hole (12:00), and two about ⅛" (3.2 mm) apart at 3:00. For the right circle: one at 11:00, to the left of the existing top hole, and two at 9:00 about ⅛" (3.2 mm) apart. Attach one 6mm jump ring to the bottom hole of each 18mm circle. Use 6mm jump rings to connect the circles through their new middle holes. Use one 6mm jump ring to attach the top circle to the 22mm jump ring just above the vinyl rings. Use one 6mm jump ring to attach the bottom circle to the 22mm jump ring just below the vinyl rings. Use one

6mm jump ring to attach one 6mm glass donut to the remaining new hole of the top circle. Repeat to add one 6mm glass donut to the remaining new hole of the bottom circle.

8 Cut 2" (5 cm) of each color chain. Use one 9mm purple jump ring to string the first 6mm glass donut used in Step 7, the 10mm glass donut, the second 6mm glass donut used in Step 7, and one end of the purple chain. Use one 6mm jump ring to attach one end of the blue chain to the remaining hole of the top circle. Use one 6mm jump ring to attach one end of the turquoise chain to the remaining hole of the bottom circle.

9 Thread the MyElements donut onto the purple piece of chain from Step 7. Use one 6mm jump ring to attach 1 hole of the donut to the blue chain, 4 links from the attached end. Use one 6mm jump ring to attach the other hole of the donut to the turquoise chain, 4 links from the attached end. Attach one 9mm turquoise jump ring to the other ends of the 3 chains. Use three 6mm jump rings to attach the turquoise jump ring to 1 hole of the rotary link. Use one 6mm jump ring to attach 1 assorted glass dangle to each of the next 3 holes on both sides of the hole just used on the rotary link.

10 Use two 6mm jump rings to attach the remaining purple chain to the rotary link just opposite the first hole used. Use two 6mm jump rings to attach the remaining turquoise chain to the rotary link on the hole above the first hole used in this step. Use two 6mm jump rings to attach the remaining blue chain to the rotary link on the hole below the first hole used in this step. Use one 9mm purple jump ring to attach the other ends of the chain and the remaining 6mm glass donut to the eye half of the clasp. Use one 9mm purple jump ring to attach the 3 chains about 2" (5 cm) (11 links) from the end of the chains. Use the remaining 9mm jump ring to attach the hook to the other ends of the chain.

artifacts

Jane Dickerson

The beautiful lampworked beads in this necklace look like they were excavated from an ancient ruin—each has a unique texture and design. Paired with copper and black chain, the best of each bead is revealed.

MATERIALS

10" (25.5 cm) of antiqued copper 6mm rolo chain

7½" (19 cm) of black 10×8mm cable chain

12 assorted JoAnne Zekowski 10–20mm lampworked glass beads

12 antiqued copper 8mm jump rings

2 antiqued copper 10mm jump rings

12" (30.5 cm) of copper 16-gauge wire

1 antiqued copper 18mm lobster clasp

TOOLS

Round-nose pliers
2 pairs of chain-nose pliers

Flush cutters

Finished size: 27¾" (70.5 cm)

Copper chain, jump rings, and lobster clasp: The Bead Empire. Black chain: AD Adornments. Lampworked glass beads: JoAnne Zekowski.

1 Cut two 3½" (9 cm) and two 1½" (4 cm) pieces of copper chain. Cut three 2½" (6 cm) pieces of black chain.

2 Use 2" (5 cm) of wire to form a simple loop. String 1 lampworked glass bead and form a simple loop. Repeat five times, stringing 1 to 3 lampworked glass beads onto each wire.

3 Attach one 10mm jump ring to the end of one 3½" (9 cm) piece of copper chain. Use one 8mm jump ring to attach the other end of the chain to one end of 1 beaded link. Use one 8mm jump ring to attach the other end of the link to one end of 1 piece of black chain.

4 Use one 8mm jump ring to attach the other end of the black chain to 1 beaded link. Use one 8mm jump ring to attach the other end of the link to one 1½" (4 cm) piece of copper chain. Use one 8mm jump ring to attach the other end of the chain to 1 beaded link. Use one 8mm jump ring to attach the other end of the link to one end of 1 piece of black chain.

5 Repeat Step 4. Use one 8mm jump ring to attach the other end of the black chain to 1 beaded link. Use one 8mm jump ring to attach the other end of the link to one end of the other 3½" (9 cm) piece of copper chain. Use one 10mm jump ring to attach the other end of the chain to the lobster clasp.

go for baroque

Denise Peck

The baroque shell design on this polymer focal is beautiful. And, it's two sided, eliminating the concern that it may turn over. A single extension of chain makes the size adjustable, and the charms keep it weighted so it sits properly on your wrist.

MATERIALS

22½" (57 cm) of base metal 5×8mm oval link chain

1½" (4 cm) polymer focal link

4 assorted 8–20mm silver charms

4 head pins (if necessary for the charms)

14mm simple hook clasp

TOOLS

2 pairs of chain-nose pliers

Flush cutters

Finished size: 7" (18 cm)

Polymer focal: ExpeditionD. Chain: Michaels. Charms: Hands of the Hills.

1 Cut the chain into six 3½" (9 cm) pieces and one 1½" (3.8 cm) piece.

2 Use chain-nose pliers to attach the end links of 3 chain lengths to one side of the focal. Repeat with the other 3 chain lengths on the other side of the focal.

3 Remove 2 links from the 1½" (3.8 cm) chain from Step 1 to use as jump rings. Gather the 3 end links on one side of the bracelet and use 1 jump ring to attach chain ends to the hook side of the clasp.

4 Gather the remaining 3 end links and use 1 jump ring to attach the chain ends to one end of the remaining 1½" (3.8 cm) chain (the extender).

5 Add the charms on every other link of the extender, either by opening the link and slipping them on, or using head pins where needed and connecting those with wire-wrapped loops.

best of both worlds

Denise Peck

Combine a collection of beads on a length of 16-gauge wire, add a triple chain section, and you have a bracelet that's both a bangle and a charm bracelet. Add charms to the chain to embellish it even more.

MATERIALS

10½" (26.5 cm) of sterling silver 3×5mm oval cable chain

8 assorted 10–14mm glass, porcelain, and metal beads

2 Bali silver 10×15mm end cones

4" (10 cm) of sterling silver 16-gauge half-hard round wire

4" (10 cm) of sterling silver 20-gauge dead-soft round wire

1 sterling silver 8mm jump ring

1 sterling silver hook clasp

TOOLS

Round-nose pliers

2 pairs of chain-nose pliers

Flush cutters

Finished size: 7¾" (19.5 cm)

Clay beads: Keith O'Connor. Matte glass beads: Zippybeads. Sterling and copper beads and sterling chain: Multi Creations, NJ. Sterling end cones: Hands of the Hills.

1 Use the 16-gauge wire to form a simple loop that attaches to the hook clasp. Use the wire to string the 8 assorted beads and form a simple loop.

2 Cut the chain into three 3½" (9 cm) pieces.

3 Use 2" (5 cm) of 20-gauge wire to form a simple loop that attaches to one end of each chain. Use the wire to string 1 cone and form a wrapped loop that attaches to the second simple loop formed in Step 1.

4 Use 2" (5 cm) of 20-gauge wire to form a simple loop that attaches to the other ends of the chains. Use the wire to string 1 cone and form a wrapped loop that attaches to the jump ring.

tiptoe through
the tulips
Lorelei Eurto

The large chain links on one side and the small wire-wrapped sections of seed beads up the other side draw your eye up and around the necklace. Using smaller cable chain at the back of the necklace makes it more comfortable to wear.

MATERIALS

3 links of silver-tone 18mm chain

6¾" (17 cm) of silver-tone cable chain

1 ceramic 35×50mm tulip pendant

2 flat purple 7×10mm lampworked beads

3 purple 4–5mm round glass beads

1 purple 1⅜" (3.5 cm) glass tube bead

4 new jade 5×7mm rondelles

100 purple size 11° seed beads

30 silver-lined yellow size 11° seed beads

55 matte purple and yellow size 11° seed beads

2 purple bugle beads

6 silver 5–6mm daisy spacers

3 silver 2" (5 cm) head pins

5 silver 5–6mm oval jump rings

9" (23 cm) of silver 22-gauge artistic wire

30" (76 cm) of silver 26-gauge artistic wire

1 silver 25mm S-clasp

TOOLS

Round-nose pliers

2 pairs of chain-nose pliers

Flush cutters

Finished size: 19½" (49.5 cm)

Ceramic tulip pendant: Gaea. Lampworked glass beads: Guy Melamed. S-clasp: Cindy Hoo. Jade, round glass beads, and silver spacers: Emmi Beads. Chain, artistic wire, and findings: Michaels. Glass tube bead: Sunyno.

1 Use 1 head pin to string 1 purple round glass bead. Form a wrapped loop that attaches to the bottom loop of the ceramic pendant. Repeat entire step twice.

2 Use 2 oval jump rings to attach two 18mm chain links. Use 2 oval jump rings to attach the third 18mm chain link to the previous link. Use 1 oval jump ring to attach the third link to the top loop of the pendant. Set aside.

3 Use 2" (5 cm) of 26-gauge wire to form a wrapped loop. String 5 purple seed beads, 3 silver-lined yellow seed beads, and 5 purple seed beads. Form a wrapped loop.

4 Repeat Step 3 four times, attaching the first wrapped loop of each new wire to the previous wrapped loop, thereby forming a chain of seed-bead links.

5 Repeat Steps 3 and 4 for a second chain.

6 Use 2" (5 cm) of 26-gauge wire to form a wrapped loop. String 13 assorted matte purple and yellow seed beads. Form a wrapped loop.

7 Use 2" (5 cm) of 26-gauge wire to form a wrapped loop that attaches to the previous wrapped loop. String 4 matte yellow seed beads, 1 bugle bead, and 4 matte yellow seed beads. Form a wrapped loop.

8 Repeat Steps 6 and 7, attaching the first wrapped loop of a new wire to the previous wrapped loop. Repeat Step 6 to form a chain of seed-bead links.

9 Cut 3" (8 cm) of 22-gauge wire. Form a wrapped loop that attaches to the top loop of the pendant. String 1 daisy spacer, the purple glass tube, and 1 daisy spacer. Form a wrapped loop that attaches to one end of each of the 3 chains formed in Steps 3 to 8.

10 Cut 3" (8 cm) of 22-gauge wire. Form a wrapped loop that attaches to the other ends of the 3 chains. String 1 jade rondelle, 1 daisy spacer, 1 lampworked bead, 1 daisy spacer, and 1 jade rondelle. Form a wrapped loop that attaches to one end of the cable chain.

11 Repeat Step 10, attaching the first wrapped loop to the other end of the chain and attaching the second wrapped loop to the S-clasp.

open doors

Denise Peck

Mary Cullinan's whimsical raku beads are a delight—little clay houses, and pendants she calls doors. It's a natural to put them together in one necklace and simple when you use chain!

MATERIALS

21" (53 cm) of sterling silver hammered cable chain

4 raku 10×12–10×20mm house beads

1 raku 10×35mm door bead

18" (46 cm) of sterling silver 20-gauge wire

TOOLS

Round-nose pliers

Chain-nose pliers

Flush cutters

Ball-peen hammer

Steel bench block

Finished size: 25" (63.5 cm)

Chain: Multi Creations, NJ. Raku beads and pendant: Jubilee.

1 Cut the 20-gauge wire into five 3" (8 cm) pieces.

2 Make a simple loop on one end of 1 piece of wire. String 1 house bead and form a simple loop. Carefully hammer both simple loops flat with the hammer and bench block. *Caution:* Be careful to stay clear of the clay bead!

3 Repeat Step 2 with the other 3 houses. Open the simple loop at the top of one house and connect it to one end link on the chain. Open the top link of another house and connect it to the bottom loop of the previous house. Continue until all the houses are connected to each other. Connect the last loop of the last house to the other end of the chain.

4 Hammer flat the last 3" (8 cm) piece of wire and thread it through the top of the door pendant. Center the wire within the pendant and bend each end straight up against the edge of the pendant. With round-nose pliers, make a simple loop on each end of the wire.

5 Open the simple loops on the pendant and connect them to 1 link of the chain, 1½" (4 cm) down from the bottom house. Close the loops.

totally tubular

Denise Peck

These beautiful raku tube beads add an unusual and dramatic flare to this chain necklace. No clasp is necessary; just slip it over your head.

MATERIALS

26" (66 cm) of antiqued brass 8mm oval cable chain

7" (18 cm) of antiqued brass 6mm textured round link chain

3 raku 1¾" (4 cm) tube beads

1 raku 2½" (6 cm) link bead

7½" (19 cm) of copper 20-gauge wire

2 copper 5mm jump rings

TOOLS

Round-nose pliers

2 pairs of chain-nose pliers

Flush cutters

Finished size: 34½" (88 cm)

Chain: AD Adornments. Raku beads: Lisa Peters Art.

1 Cut the 20-gauge wire into three 2½" (6 cm) pieces. Cut the cable chain into one 17" (43 cm) piece, one 7" (18 cm) piece, and two 1" (2.5 cm) pieces.

2 Use 1 jump ring to attach one end of the link bead to one end each of the round link chain and the 7" (18 cm) piece of cable chain. Use 1 jump ring to attach the other ends of the chains. Use 1 piece of wire to form a simple loop that attaches to the jump ring. String 1 tube bead and form a simple loop that attaches to one 1" (2.5 cm) chain.

3 Use 1 piece of wire to form a simple loop that attaches to the other end of the chain. String 1 tube bead and form a simple loop that attaches to the other 1" (2.5 cm) chain. Use 1 piece of wire to form a simple loop that attaches to the other end of the chain. String 1 tube bead and form a simple loop that attaches to one end of the 17" (43 cm) chain. Attach the other end of the chain to the other end of the link bead.

high wire act

Kerry Bogert

This design is a twist on the classic pendant idea. Instead of hanging the pendant down, why not flip it on its side? Throw in some mix-and-match chain, toss it up with colorful beads, and you have a recipe for fun.

1. Wrap the purple-colored wire tightly around the mandrel until you have a 1" (2.5 cm) coil. Trim the ends of the wire and slide your coil off the mandrel. Repeat with the dark green wire. Repeat with the lime-colored wire except make a ½" (13 mm) coil.

2. Use the 18-gauge wire to make a wrapped loop large enough for the rolo chain to slide through easily. String the green 15mm disc, the purple hollow bead, the lime green coil, the green-and-blue 24mm disc, the green hollow bead, and the blue 15mm glass disc. Form a wrapped loop.

3. Cut the rolo chain into two 10" (25 cm) pieces. Cut the 20-gauge wire in half. Cut the cable chain into two 3" (8 cm) pieces.

4. Use 1 piece of chain to string the wrapped loop next to the green 15mm disc. Use one end of the chain to string the purple wire coil and the blue-and-white polka dot glass ring. Use the other end of the chain to string the blue bubble bead. Use 1 wire to form a wrapped loop that attaches to both ends of the rolo chain. Use the other end of the wire to form a wrapped loop that attaches to one end of 1 piece of cable chain. Attach the hook half of the clasp to the other end of the cable chain.

5. Repeat Step 4 for the other half of the necklace, using the green wire coil, the purple glass ring, and the green bubble bead. Attach the eye half of the clasp to the end of the cable chain.

MATERIALS

20" (50 cm) of sterling silver 2.1mm rolo chain

6" (15 cm) of sterling silver 3.7mm flat cable chain

1 purple 22mm hollow round lampworked glass bead

1 green 22mm hollow round lampworked glass bead

1 green-and-blue 24mm large-hole lampworked glass disc

1 green 10mm lampworked glass bubble bead

1 blue 10mm lampworked glass bubble bead

1 purple 20mm lampworked glass ring

1 blue-and-white polka dot 20mm lampworked glass ring

1 green 15mm lampworked glass disc

1 blue 15mm lampworked glass disc

10" (25 cm) of sterling silver 20-gauge wire

8" (20 cm) of sterling silver 18-gauge wire

12–18" (30–46 cm) each of 20-gauge colored copper wire in purple, green, and seafoam

1 sterling silver S-clasp

TOOLS

Round-nose pliers

2 pairs of chain-nose pliers

Flush cutters

⅜" (9.5 mm) mandrel

Finished size: 20" (51 cm)

Lampworked beads and S-clasp: Kerry Bogert, Kab's Creative Concepts. Colored copper wire: Parawire. Chain: Rio Grande.

silk road

Leslie Rogalski

The warm earth tones of these wood beads look beautiful against the copper chain. Adding the dangles at just the right spot on the chain allows for maximum movement of the pieces.

MATERIALS

6" (15 cm) of bright copper 12×9mm heavy curb chain

7 terra-cotta 14×5mm wood saucer beads

8 purple 8×3mm wood saucer beads

6 green 6×3mm wood saucer beads

21 black size 8° seed beads

21 copper 2" (5 cm) head pins

21 copper 8mm jump rings

1 copper hook

TOOLS

Round-nose pliers

2 pairs of chain-nose pliers

Flush cutters

Finished size: 7" (18 cm)

Wood beads: Silk Road Treasures. Chain: ABeadstore. Jump rings, seed beads, and head pins: Check your local bead store.

1 Use 1 head pin to string 1 seed bead and 1 wood bead; form a wrapped loop. Repeat twenty times for a total of 21 dangles.

2 Lay out the chain so it is flat and even. Find the approximate middle of the chain. Use 1 jump ring to attach 1 terra-cotta dangle around the intersection of the 2 center links. All terra-cotta dangles will be added to link intersections, capturing 2 links.

3 Working with the 2 links from Step 2, attach 1 purple dangle to the top of the left link. Attach 1 green dangle to the bottom of the right link.

4 Repeat this pattern along the length of the chain, working from the middle to one end, then working the other side of the chain. There should be a few loose links at both ends.

5 Attach the hook clasp to the end link on one end of the bracelet. Use the free link at the other end of the bracelet as the ring for the hook.

beach stones

Jane Dickerson

These rich gray stones are silky smooth to the touch and remind me of the kind we used to skip across the water when we were kids. They are gathered from the beaches in Lake Michigan and beautifully polished by nature.

MATERIALS

10" (25 cm) of sterling silver 5mm rolo chain

4 dark gray 12×22mm beach stones

21 sterling silver 8mm 18-gauge jump rings

1 sterling silver 10mm toggle clasp with extender chain

TOOLS

2 pairs of chain-nose pliers

Flush cutters

Liver of sulfur

0000 extra-fine steel wool

Finished size: 7½" (19 cm)

Beach stones: Riverstone Bead Company. Chain, jump rings, and liver of sulfur: Rio Grande. Clasp: Nina Designs. Steel wool: Home Depot.

1 Clean and oxidize all the silver. See page 21 for oxidizing instructions. Remove the excess patina with steel wool.

2 Cut sixteen 3-link pieces of chain. Open 1 jump ring; attach the extender chain on the toggle clasp to the end links of 2 pieces of chain. Close the jump ring.

3 Use 1 jump ring to attach the other end of 1 chain to one hole of 1 beach stone. Use 1 jump ring to attach the other end of the other chain to the other hole of the beach stone.

4 Use 1 jump ring to attach one end of 1 chain to one hole of the beach stone. Use 1 jump ring to attach one end of another chain to the other hole of the beach stone. Use 1 jump ring to connect the other ends of the 2 chains to one end of each of 2 new chains.

5 Repeat Steps 3 and 4 three times, replacing the final 2 chains with the ring half of the clasp.

bicycle chain

Jane Dickerson

The inspiration for this bracelet came from Nyssa Lyon of hourglassproductions.etsy.com. I purchased a fantastic bicycle-chain bracelet from her and asked her permission to re-create one for the book. Mine is slightly different, but her idea to recycle the bicycle for jewelry was too good to pass up!

MATERIALS

6 copper ³⁄₁₆" (8 mm) washers

5 bicycle-chain links

20 antique copper 16×3mm figure-eight connectors

2" (5 cm) of 16-gauge copper wire

TOOLS

Round-nose pliers

2 pairs of chain-nose pliers

Flush cutters

Ball-peen hammer

Steel bench block

Finished size: 7¼" (18 cm)

Bicycle-chain links: The Wishing Bead. Copper washers: Harbor Freight. Antique copper connectors: Gems and Findings. Copper wire and tools: Metalliferous.

1. Use the round end of the ball-peen hammer and a steel bench block to hammer the top of all the copper washers to texture them.

2. Use chain-nose pliers to open 1 loop on a connector and close it around 1 washer. Make sure you have the textured side up. Repeat with a second connector, attaching it to the same washer. Open the loops on the opposite end of the connectors and attach them to the top and bottom holes of the bicycle-chain link.

3. Open 1 loop on a connector and attach it to the top loop of the bicycle link in Step 2. Repeat with a second connector on the bottom of the bicycle link. Attach the ends of both connectors to 1 washer. Repeat Steps 2 and 3, connecting the washers and bicycle-chain links together, ending with a washer.

4. Use the copper wire to make an S-hook clasp (see page 21 for instructions). For a slight variation on the one shown, flatten the tips of both ends of the wire into a little paddle before creating the initial loops on the ends of the clasp. This just adds a little extra to the traditional clasp.

brass rings

Jane Dickerson

When I was a little girl, my sisters and I visited a park with a gorgeous old merry-go-round. If you could grab a brass ring as the carousel went around, you would win a free ride. This necklace is a reminder of those days. And guess what? All the materials came from the hardware store!

MATERIALS

1 brass 32mm washer

28 brass 11mm washers

2 brass 9mm washers

6 brass 7mm washers

2 copper 16mm jump rings

30 copper 13mm jump rings

1 copper 10mm jump ring

1 copper hook clasp

18-gauge copper wire (optional)

TOOLS

2 pairs of chain-nose pliers

Euro Tool 2-hole metal punch

Round-nose pliers (optional)

1 Sharpie pen (optional)

Finished size: 19½" (49.5 cm)

Check your local hardware store. Euro Tool: Rings & Things.

1   Use the ³⁄₃₂" punch (large punch) on the 2-hole punch to create a circular texture on the surface of the 32mm washer. Drill the punch into the surface of the washer until a circular mark is made. Unscrew the punch and rotate the washer to place the circular mark in different spots.

2   Use readymade jump rings or create your own following the instructions on page 18. For the 13mm jump rings, use 18-gauge copper wire and a Sharpie pen as a mandrel. For the 16mm jump rings, use a round object a few millimeters larger than the Sharpie pen; any round object will do.

3   Use one 13mm jump ring to attach the hook clasp to one 11mm washer.

4   Use one 13mm jump ring to attach one 11mm washer to the previous washer. Repeat twelve times.

5   Use one 13mm jump ring to attach the previous washer to one 16mm jump ring. Attach the 16mm jump ring to the 32mm washer.

6   Attach one 13mm jump ring to one 11mm washer. Repeat Step 4. Repeat Step 5.

7   Open the 10mm jump ring and string three 7mm washers, two 9mm washers, and three 7mm washers. Attach the 10mm jump ring to both of the 16mm jump rings.

jaded machine
Melanie Brooks

This steampunk-style necklace was inspired by the mechanical workings of gears, chains, and pulleys. Mix aged brass chain with porcelain and shimmering crystals and you have a modern look with a hint of the industrial era.

MATERIALS

30" (76 cm) of natural brass 3.5mm rolo chain

5 round pewter and acid green 18mm porcelain gear links

37 faceted peridot luster 4mm fire-polished Czech glass beads

7 faceted peridot luster 3mm fire-polished Czech glass beads

1 natural brass 22mm hammered brass ring

1 natural brass 7×24mm bead pod toggle bar

2 natural brass 10mm round jump rings (large)

12 natural brass 7.25mm round jump rings (medium)

29 natural brass 4.25mm round jump rings (small)

38 natural brass 1" (2.5 cm) head pins

TOOLS

Round-nose pliers

2 pairs of chain-nose pliers

Flush cutters

Ruler

Finished size: 19" (48 cm)

Porcelain: Melanie Brooks, Earthenwood Studio. Natural brass: Vintaj Natural Brass Co. Glass beads: Fusion Beads.

1 Cut 20 lengths of chain with 11 links each. Attach 1 small jump ring to the hammered ring. Use 1 medium jump ring to attach 2 lengths of chain to the small jump ring.

2 Use 1 medium jump ring to attach the other ends of the previous 2 chains to 2 lengths of chain. Repeat three times. Attach 1 medium jump ring to the 2 end links of chain. Attach 2 small jump rings to the medium ring. Attach 1 large jump ring to the 2 small jump rings. Use 2 small jump rings to attach the large ring to 1 porcelain gear link.

3 Use 2 small jump rings to attach a new porcelain gear link to the previous one. Repeat three times. Repeat Step 2, reversing the sequence. Attach 1 medium jump ring to the 2 end links of chain. Use 2 small jump rings to attach the medium ring to the bead pod toggle bar.

4 Use 1 head pin to string the seven 3mm glass beads and insert head first into the toggle bar. Close the top end of the toggle bar with chain-nose pliers, then cut the end of the head pin flush to the top of the beads. Close the other end of the toggle bar.

5 Cut 5 lengths of chain with 13 links each. Use 1 small jump ring to attach 1 length of chain to the side loop of 1 porcelain gear link. Use 1 small jump ring to attach the other end of the chain to the other side of the link. Repeat for the other 4 porcelain links.

6 Use 1 head pin to string one 4mm glass bead. Form a small loop at the top and trim the wire. Repeat thirty-six times. Attach 1 glass bead dangle to each of the 6 medium jump rings on one side of the chain necklace. Repeat on other side.

7 Attach 1 glass bead dangle to the chain that hangs from the porcelain gear link—to the third link in the chain. Skip a link and attach another dangle to the next link; repeat to add 3 more dangles. Repeat this step, adding 5 dangles to the chain on each porcelain gear link.

one yard dash

Kerry Bogert

Versatility abounds in this design. It can be worn long or doubled—you can't go wrong. It's also a great way to use leftover beads and stray short pieces of chain.

MATERIALS

24" (61 cm) of sterling silver 2.1mm rolo chain

7" (18 cm) of sterling silver 3.9mm rolo chain

12" (30.5 cm) of sterling silver 3.7mm flat cable chain

4 assorted 20–28mm hollow lampworked glass beads

6 assorted 18–30mm large-hole lampworked glass rings; ¼–½" (6.4–12.7mm) holes

3 (8 cm) assorted 12–16mm decorative round lampworked glass beads

4 filigrana (color encased in clear) 10–20mm lampworked glass discs

6 solid color 7–18mm lampworked glass discs

8 sterling silver 4mm Smart beads

3" (8 cm) of sterling silver 16-gauge wire

24" (61 cm) of sterling silver 18-gauge wire

16" (41 cm) of sterling silver 20-gauge wire

20" (51 cm) of 20-gauge colored copper wire coiled around ³⁄₃₂" mandrel

1 turquoise 8mm aluminum jump ring

1 sterling silver toggle bar

TOOLS

Round-nose pliers

2 pairs of chain-nose pliers

Flush cutters

³⁄₃₂" (2.4 mm) mandrel

Finished size: 39" (99 cm)

Lampworked beads and toggle clasp: Kerry Bogert, Kab's Creative Concepts. Smart beads: Jewelry Supply. Chain: Rio Grande.

1 The construction of this piece comes together best when starting at one end and building your way toward the other. Set aside 1 glass ring with ½" (12.7 mm) hole. This will be used as the ring half of the clasp. Coil the entire length of the 20-gauge colored copper wire around the mandrel. Set aside.

2 Cut a 3" (8 cm) piece of flat cable chain. Use the jump ring to attach the toggle bar to one end of the chain. Cut a 4" (10 cm) piece of 18-gauge wire and form a wrapped loop that attaches to the other end of the chain. String 1 hollow bead, 1 solid color disc, and 1 Smart bead. Form a wrapped loop that attaches to 1 large-hole glass ring.

3 Cut a 4" (10 cm) piece of 2.1mm rolo chain. Cut a 4" (10 cm) piece of sterling silver 20-gauge wire and form a wrapped loop that attaches to one end of the rolo chain. String the previous glass ring and another large-hole glass ring. Form a wrapped loop that attaches to the other end of the chain, wrapping over the previous wrap for a neat double-wrapped link.

4 Cut a 5½" (14 cm) piece of flat cable chain. Pass one end of the chain through the previous glass ring and bring both ends together. Cut a 4" (10 cm) piece of 18-gauge wire and form a wrapped loop that attaches to both ends of the chain. String 1 Smart bead, 1 hollow bead, 1 Smart bead, 1 decorated round bead, and 1 solid color disc, and form a wrapped loop.

5 Cut a 6" (15 cm) piece of 2.1mm rolo chain. Cut a 4" (10 cm) piece of 20-gauge wire and form a wrapped loop that attaches to the previous wrapped loop. Cut a ¼" (6.4 mm) coil from the colored copper wire coil. Use the chain to string 1 solid color disc and the cut piece of coiled wire. Bring both ends of the chain together. Use the other end of the 20-gauge wire to form a wrapped loop that attaches both ends of the chain, wrapping over the previous wrap for a neat double-wrapped link.

6 Cut 4" (10 cm) of 18-gauge wire. Form a wrapped loop that attaches to the previous rolo chain between the disc and the wire coil. Cut a ¾" (19 mm) coil from the colored copper wire coil. Cut a 3" (8 cm) piece of 3.9mm rolo chain. String 1 Smart bead, 1 decorative round bead, the ¾" (19 mm) coil, 1 large-hole ring over the coil, 1 filigrana glass disc, and 1 Smart bead. Form a wrapped loop that attaches to one end of the chain.

7 Cut two 1½" (4 cm) pieces of 16-gauge wire. Create 2 figure-eight links (see page 19 for instructions) to attach to 1 large-hole ring. *Note:* Make sure the loops that link to the glass ring are large enough to fit around the diameter of the ring. It's okay if the other side of the loop is smaller than the part attached to the ring.

8 Use chain-nose pliers to open the larger loop of 1 figure eight and attach it to the glass ring. Open the other side of the link and attach it to the last link in the rolo chain from Step 6. Open the larger loop of the second figure eight and attach it around the opposite side of the glass ring. Cut a 3" (8 cm) piece of flat cable chain. Open the smaller loop of the second figure eight and attach it to the end link of the flat cable chain; close the link.

9 Cut a 4" (10 cm) piece of 18-gauge wire and form a wrapped loop that attaches to the other end of the previous chain. Cut a ½" (12.7 mm) coil from the colored copper wire coil. Use the 18-gauge wire to string 1 decorative round bead, the ½" (12.7 mm) coil, and 2 solid color glass discs. Form a wrapped loop.

10 Cut a 6" (15 cm) piece of 2.1mm rolo chain. Pass one end of the chain through the loop of the previous link. Bring both ends of the chain together. Cut a 4" (10 cm) piece of 20-gauge wire and form a wrapped loop that attaches to both ends of the chain. Use the other end of the wire to form a wrapped loop, wrapping over the previous wrap for a neat double-wrapped link.

11 Cut a 3" (8 cm) piece of 3.9mm rolo chain. Cut 4" (10 cm) of 18-gauge wire and form a wrapped loop that attaches to the previous wrapped loop. String 1 filigrana disc, 1 Smart bead, 1 hollow bead, 1 Smart bead, and 1 filigrana disc, and form a wrapped loop that attaches to one end link of the rolo chain.

12 Use the other end of the rolo chain to string 1 large-hole ring. Cut 4" (10 cm) of 18-gauge wire and form a wrapped loop that attaches to the end of the chain. Cut a ¼" (6.4 mm) coil from the colored copper wire coil. Use the 18-gauge wire to string 1 glass disc, the ¼" (6.4 mm) coil, 1 Smart bead, 1 hollow glass bead, and 1 solid color disc, and form a wrapped loop.

13 Cut 6" (15 cm) of 2.1mm rolo chain. Cut 4" (10 cm) of 20-gauge wire and form a wrapped loop that attaches to one end of the rolo chain. Use the chain to string the previous wrapped loop and the large glass ring set aside from Step 1. Use the other end of the wire to form a wrapped loop that attaches to the other end of the chain, wrapping over the previous wrapped loop for a neat double-wrapped link.

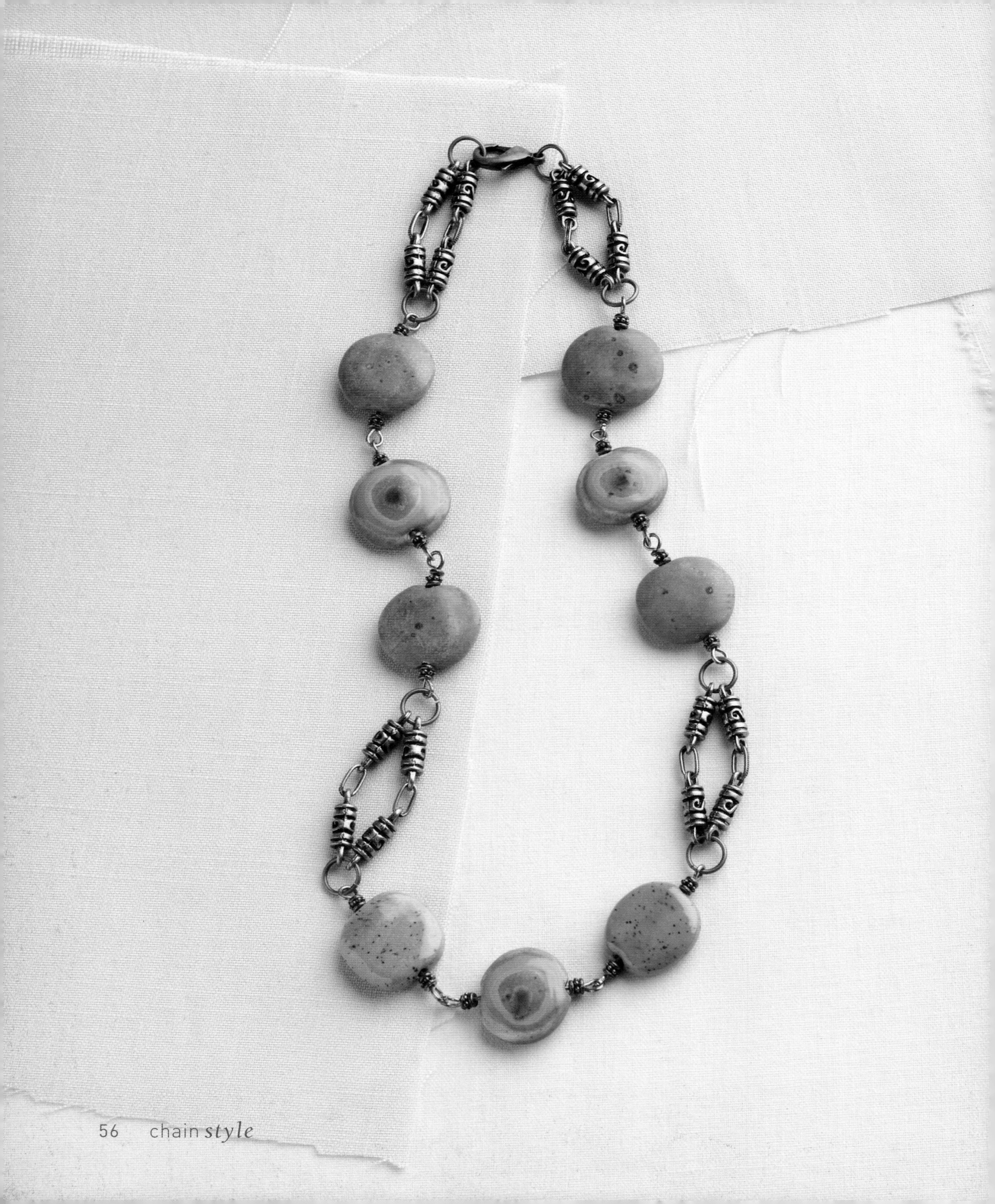

cartwheels

Jane Dickerson

The beads in this necklace are called Happy Beads! Who wouldn't want a necklace with that kind of ingredient? They come in loads of colors, but I chose earth tones because they complement this great textured copper chain.

MATERIALS

16" (40.5 cm) of antique copper 10×5mm barrel link chain

9 ceramic 22–24mm Happy Beads

8 antique copper 10mm jump rings

1 antique copper 15mm lobster clasp

36 antique copper 3mm flat spacers

18 antique copper 3mm heishi

8 antique copper 10mm jump rings

18" (45.5 cm) of copper 18-gauge wire

TOOLS

Round-nose pliers

2 pairs of chain-nose pliers

Flush cutters

Finished size: 22½" (57 cm)

Chain, clasp, and jump rings: Bead Empire.
Happy Beads: Some Enchanted Beading.
Spacers and heishi: Tierra Cast.

---

1 Use 2" (5 cm) of wire to form a simple loop. String 1 flat spacer, 1 heishi, 1 flat spacer, 1 Happy Bead, 1 flat spacer, 1 heishi spacer, and 1 flat spacer. Form a simple loop.

2 Repeat Step 1 twice, attaching the first loop of the step to the previous loop.

3 Repeat Steps 1 and 2 twice for a total of 3 beaded sections.

4 Separate the chain into 8 sections, each with 2 barrels connected by an oval link between.

5 Use 1 jump ring to attach 1 lobster clasp to one end of each of 2 chain sections. Use 1 jump ring to attach the other ends of the chain sections to one end of 1 beaded section.

6 Use 1 jump ring to attach the other end of the beaded section to one end of each of 2 chain sections. Use 1 jump ring to attach the other ends of the chain sections to one end of 1 beaded section.

7 Repeat Step 6 twice, omitting the final beaded section.

so soho
Lorelei Eurto

The chunky beads and dark tones paired with the heavy brass cable chain add to the bohemian, hippy feel of this necklace. The filigree ring mimics the round shape of the polymer clay disc on the opposite side of the necklace.

MATERIALS

9" (23 cm) of brass 6–8mm double-linked cable chain

1 brown rectangle 25×40mm wood frame focal bead

3 brown carved 10–12mm oval wood beads

1 light brown 10mm round wood bead

1 flat brown 18mm square wood bead

2 red 4×12mm nut disc beads

1 striped 7×15mm coconut bead

1 polymer clay 25mm disc bead

1 green dimpled 12mm ceramic round bead

8 green faceted 4×6mm Czech glass rondelles

1 brass 22mm filigree ring

2 brass 3–4mm cubes

2 brass 8mm etched jump rings

1 brass 6mm jump ring

6" (15 cm) of .018 beading wire

6" (15 cm) of brass 24-gauge wire

3½" (9 cm) of brass 22-gauge wire

2 brass crimp beads

1 brass 23mm hook clasp

TOOLS

Round-nose pliers

2 pairs of chain-nose pliers

Crimping pliers

Flush cutters

Finished size: 18¾" (47.5 cm)

Beading wire, brass chain, and wood beads: Michaels, Hobby Lobby. Carved wood ovals and coconut beads: Terrestrial—Beads with Culture. Dimpled ceramic bead: Stefanie Meisel, Distracted Muse. Czech glass: Emmi Beads. Nut discs beads: Sunyno. All Vintaj brass: Fusion Beads. Brass wire: Patina Queen. Polymer disc bead: Humblebeads.

1   Cut two 3" (7.5 cm) sections of 24-gauge wire. Fold one wire in half tightly. Thread both cut ends together through the hole in the center of the polymer disc bead. Pull the loop side of the wire toward the edge of the disc until ¼" (6 mm) of the loop is showing above the edge. Hold that side of the wire flat against the disc and fold the other side (the two cut ends) up to touch the loop. Take the left cut wire and wrap it four times around the loop, trim the end, and tuck in the tail with chain-nose pliers. Wrap the right wire around the existing wrap four times, creating a double-wrapped loop. Trim the excess wire and tuck in the end.

2   Take the remaining piece of 24-gauge wire and thread one end through the hole of the disc bead, sliding the bead to the center of the wire. Bend each end upward to the edge of the disc bead, directly opposite the wire in Step 1. Create a wrapped loop with one of the wires, wrapping the wire around four times. Trim the wrapped wire and tuck in the end. Take the other wire and wrap it around the previous wrap, creating a nice double-wrapped loop. Set aside the polymer link.

3   Use the 22-gauge wire to form a wrapped loop that attaches to the hook clasp. String 1 faceted rondelle, the first hole of the wood frame focal bead, 6 faceted rondelle beads, the second hole of the wood frame focal bead, and 1 faceted rondelle. Form a wrapped loop that attaches to 1 etched jump ring. Attach the jump ring to the filigree ring. Attach the other etched jump ring to the filigree ring.

4   Use the beading wire to string 1 crimp bead and the previous etched jump ring. Pass back through the crimp bead and crimp. String 1 brass cube bead, the dimpled ceramic bead, the light brown wood bead, 1 red disc bead, the flat square bead, 1 red disc bead, the coconut bead, 3 carved wood ovals, 1 brass cube bead, 1 crimp bead, and the wrapped loop from the polymer link. Pass back through the crimp bead and crimp.

5   Use the 6mm jump ring to attach the other end of the polymer link to one end of the chain. Hook the clasp onto the other end of the chain.

chain *style*

copper fusion

Jane Dickerson

The three copper chains used in this necklace each have a different shape and texture: shiny and round, oval and antiqued. Finish it off with a fabulous shibuichi toggle and you'll look like a million bucks in about 15 minutes!

MATERIALS

16½" (42 cm) of antiqued copper 15×8mm elongated oval cable chain

16½" (42 cm) of antiqued copper 8×5mm flat oval cable chain

16½" (42 cm) of bright copper 10mm cable chain

2 antique copper 10mm jump rings

1 shibu 35mm Saki Silver toggle clasp

TOOLS

2 chain-nose pliers

Flush cutters

Finished size: 17" (43 cm)

Elongated oval chain: Rosalyn Designs. Flat oval chain: Out on a Whim. 10mm cable chain: Chelsea's Beads. Shibu toggle clasp (style: ss63): Saki Silver. Jump rings: The Bead Empire.

1 Use one 10mm jump ring to attach one end of each chain to the bar half of the clasp.

2 Repeat Step 1, attaching the chains to the ring half of the clasp.

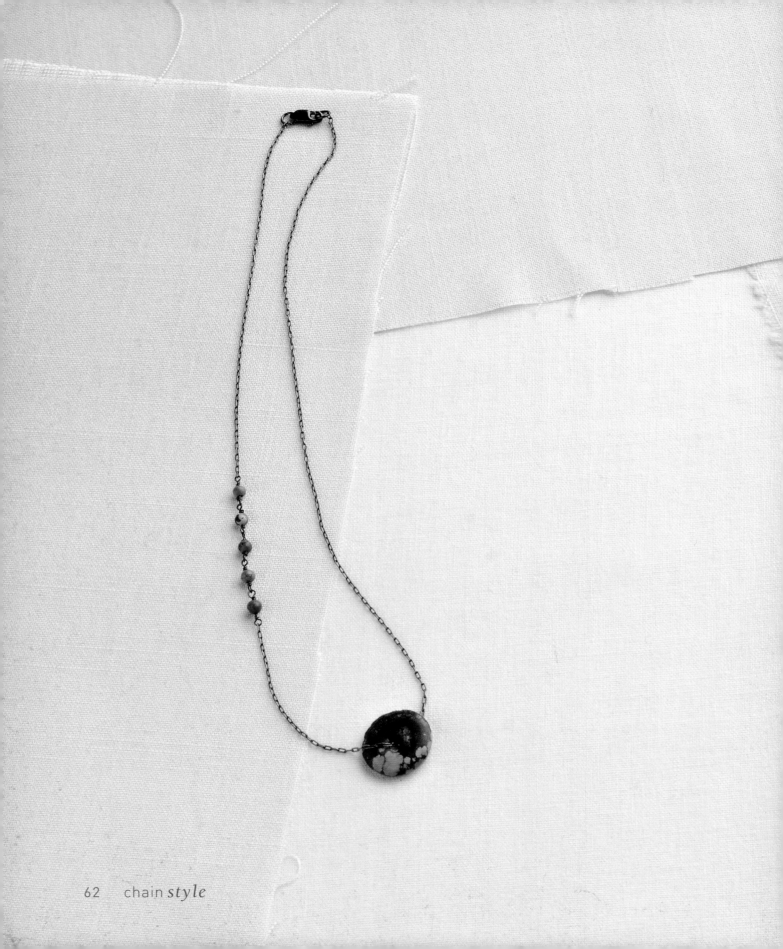

delicate donut

Denise Peck

The nice thing about making jewelry is that just changing the scale of some basic techniques will produce a whole different look. This very fine chain is embellished with 4mm round turquoise beads and then strung with one small turquoise donut. Big impact with tiny beads!

MATERIALS

17" (43 cm) of sterling silver 2×1mm cable chain (13 links per inch)

5 turquoise 4mm round beads

1 turquoise 18mm donut

2 sterling silver 5mm jump rings

1 sterling silver 10×5mm lobster clasp

7½" (19 cm) of sterling silver 26-gauge dead-soft wire

TOOLS

Round-nose pliers

2 pairs of chain-nose pliers

Flush cutters

Liver of sulfur

0000 extra-fine steel wool

Finished size: 19½" (49.5 cm)

Chain: Metalliferous. 4mm turquoise beads, turquoise donut, jump rings, and lobster clasp: Fire Mountain Gems and Beads. Liver of sulfur: Rio Grande. Steel wool: Home Depot.

1 Oxidize all the sterling elements (see page 21 for instructions). Remove the excess patina with extra-fine steel wool.

2 Cut the chain into one 12" (30.5 cm) piece and one 5" (13 cm) piece. Use 1 jump ring to attach the lobster clasp to one end of the 5" (13 cm) chain. Use 1½" (4 cm) of wire to form a wrapped loop that attaches to the other end of the chain. String 1 turquoise bead and form a wrapped loop.

3 Use 1½" (4 cm) of wire to form a wrapped loop that attaches to the previous wrapped loop. String 1 turquoise bead and form a wrapped loop.

4 Repeat Step 3 three times, attaching the final wrapped loop to one end of the 12" (30.5 cm) chain. Use the chain to string the donut. Attach the remaining jump ring to the other end of the chain.

filigree flight

Melanie Brooks

Inspired by butterflies and winged things found fluttering in a deep woodland world, this necklace is fit for a Fairy Queen. It is so full of texture and interest, one could tell tales about it forever.

MATERIALS

25" (63.5 cm) of natural brass 4×6.5mm ladder chain

1 desert pine 24mm triple moth porcelain cabochon

2 desert pine 16mm butterfly wreath porcelain links

2 desert pine 15mm moth flower porcelain links

2 desert pine 12mm tiny butterfly porcelain links

2 desert pine 12mm tiny butterfly porcelain charms

20 copper color 4mm glass pearls

10 natural brass 6mm flower spacer beads

10 natural brass 1" head pins

3 natural brass 16×30mm nouveau connectors

1 natural brass 35mm filigree violet flower

55 natural brass 4.75mm jump rings

1 natural brass 13×17mm busy bee charm

1 natural brass 18×20mm Queen Bee connector

1 natural brass 21×6mm tiny hook clasp

TOOLS

Round-nose pliers

2 pairs of chain-nose pliers

Flush cutters

Ruler

Finished size: 18½" (47 cm)

Porcelain: Melanie Brooks, Earthenwood Studio. Natural brass: Vintaj Natural Brass Co. Glass pearls: Fusion Beads.

1　Center the porcelain cabochon onto the filigree violet flower. The metal flower petals should be facing 12:00, 2:00, 4:00, 6:00, 8:00, and 10:00. With your fingers, fold the petal at 12:00 up around the cabochon. Skip one petal (2:00) and fold up the next petal (4:00), skip one petal (6:00) and fold up the next petal (8:00), and skip the next petal (10:00). Using chain-nose pliers, press each of the folded petals down around the cabochon to hold it securely in place.

2　Using round-nose pliers, curl the end of the nouveau connector up at the narrow end to form a loop. Attach 1 jump ring to the loop. Use 2 jump rings to attach the previous jump ring to 1 tiny butterfly charm. Use 2 jump rings to attach the top of the nouveau connector to the bottom of the filigree violet.

3　Use 2 jump rings to attach the 2:00 petal of the filigree violet flower to the bottom loop in 1 butterfly wreath link. Use 2 jump rings to attach the top loop of the butterfly wreath link to the bottom loop of the moth flower link. Use 2 jump rings to attach the top loop of the moth flower link to the bottom loop of the tiny butterfly link. Use 2 jump rings to attach the top loop of the butterfly link to the wide center of 1 nouveau connector.

4　Using round-nose pliers, curl the end of the nouveau connector up at the narrow end to form a loop. Attach 1 jump ring to the loop. Cut a 6" (15 cm) length of chain. Use 2 jump rings to attach the previous jump ring to the end loop of the chain.

5　Cut a 5-link piece of chain. Use 1 jump ring to attach one side of the chain to the top loop of the butterfly wreath link. Attach 1 jump ring to the other end of the chain. Use 1 jump ring to attach the previous jump ring (at end of the chain) to the bottom loop of the butterfly wreath link.

6　Repeat Step 5 with the moth flower link. Cut a 4-link piece of chain. Repeat Step 5 with the 4-link piece of chain (instead of 5-link) and attach it to the tiny butterfly link.

7　Repeat Steps 3 to 6 for the other half of the necklace, beginning by attaching the 10:00 petal of the filigree violet flower to the bottom loop of the butterfly wreath link.

8　Cut a 7-link piece of chain. Using 1 jump ring, attach the end of the chain to the inner corner of the nouveau connector on the right. Attach 1 jump ring to the other end of the chain. Use 1 jump ring to attach the previous jump ring to the side loop of the Queen Bee connector. Repeat entire step on the other side of the necklace. Use 1 jump ring to attach 1 tiny butterfly charm to the bottom of the Queen Bee connector.

9　Use 1 head pin to string 1 pearl, 1 flower spacer, and 1 pearl, and form a simple loop. Repeat nine times to create the pearl dangles. Attach 1 pearl dangle to the outer corner of the nouveau connector on the right. Attach 1 pearl dangle to jump ring that faces out under the tiny butterfly link. Attach 1 pearl dangle to the jump ring that faces out under the moth flower link. Attach 1 pearl dangle to the jump ring that faces out under the butterfly wreath link. Attach 1 pearl dangle to the jump ring at the end of the chain next to the Queen Bee connector. Repeat these pearl dangles on the other side of the necklace.

10　Use 1 jump ring to attach one end of the necklace to the hook clasp. Cut a 1" (2.5 cm) length of chain. Use 1 jump ring to attach the 1" (2.5 cm) chain to the other end of the necklace. Use 1 jump ring to attach the busy bee charm to the end of the short chain.

chain *style*

just a bit

Jane Dickerson

The first time I remember seeing a horse bit in fashion design was on men's black Gucci shoes. This was the status shoe to wear if you were a businessman in New York or Washington, D.C., years ago, and still is. The black links in this necklace are my version of the horse bit, and a little flash from the past.

MATERIALS

9" (23 cm) of silver finish patterned 12×9mm oval long and short chain

8" (20 cm) of black 2.5mm rubber tubing

18" (46 cm) of silver 16-gauge wire (silver over copper)

1 sterling silver 18.7mm lobster clasp

TOOLS

Round-nose pliers

2 pairs of chain-nose pliers

Flush cutters

Scissors

Finished size: 18" (46 cm)

Chain: Chelsea's Beads. Rubber tubing: Beadalon. Lobster clasp: Rio Grande.

1   Each oval link on the chain is attached to the next oval link with three 8mm jump rings. Remove the middle jump ring, leaving 1 oval link with 1 jump ring attached to each side. Set the extra jump rings aside. Remove 6 oval link sections of chain with 1 oval link and 1 jump ring attached to each side.

2   Use scissors to cut eight 1" (2.5 cm) pieces of rubber tubing. Using flush cutters, cut eight 2¼" (6 cm) pieces of 16-gauge wire.

3   Use 1 wire to form a simple loop that attaches to one 8mm jump ring (left over from separating the chain in

Step 1), using the large end of your round-nose pliers. String 1 rubber tube and form a simple loop that attaches to the end of one section of chain.

4   Use 1 wire to form a simple loop that attaches to the other end of the previous section of chain. String 1 rubber tube and form a simple loop that attaches to one end of one section of chain. Repeat entire step six times, omitting the final section of chain.

5   Use one 8mm jump ring (left over from separating the chain in Step 1) to attach the final simple loop to the lobster clasp.

stepping stone

Taya and Silvija Koschnick

A tribute to the compelling nature of asymmetry, this bracelet combines bold chains with the muted, raw quality of a simple hand-drilled rock.

MATERIALS

3½" (9 cm) of sterling silver 8×17mm flattened elongated cable chain

1¾" (4.5 cm) of sterling silver 6×8mm cable chain

1 brown double-hole rectangle river rock

3 sterling silver 5mm jump rings*

2 sterling silver 6mm jump rings*

1 sterling silver 8mm soldered jump ring

1 sterling silver 13mm lobster clasp

TOOLS

2 pairs of chain-nose pliers

Liver of sulfur

0000 extra-fine steel wool

*Adjust your jump-ring sizes based on individual river rocks as their hole sizes vary.

Finished size: 7" (18 cm)

All materials: Bead Paradise.

1 Clean and oxidize all the sterling silver (see 21 for instructions). Use the steel wool to gently remove the excess patina until you reach your desired shade.

2 Use one 6mm jump ring to attach one end of the river rock to one end of the 6×8mm cable chain. Attach one 6mm jump ring to the other side of the river rock. Use one 5mm jump ring to attach the elongated cable chain to the 6mm jump ring on the river rock.

3 Use one 5mm jump ring to attach the lobster clasp to the end of the elongated cable chain. Use one 5mm jump ring to attach the 8mm soldered jump ring to the end of the 6×8mm cable chain.

solitude

Taya and Silvija Koschnick

A single stone balances perfectly within the oval ring. The scale and weight of the chain is just right for this piece, keeping the focus on the center of the bracelet.

MATERIALS

5½" (14 cm) of sterling silver 6×8mm flattened cable chain

1 gray double-hole river rock

1 small gray single-hole river rock

1 sterling silver 22×39mm flattened oval ring

5 sterling silver 6mm jump rings*

3 sterling silver 5mm jump rings*

1 sterling silver 11mm lobster clasp

TOOLS

2 pairs of chain-nose pliers

Liver of sulfur

0000 extra-fine steel wool

Rawhide hammer

Rolling pin

*Adjust your jump-ring sizes based on individual river rocks as their hole sizes vary.

Finished size: 7¼" (18 cm)

All materials: Bead Paradise.

1   Clean and oxidize all the sterling silver (see instructions on page 21). Use the steel wool to gently remove the excess patina until you reach your desired shade.

2   Slightly dome the flattened oval with a rawhide hammer over a domed object such as a rolling pin.

3   Cut the chain into two 2¾" (7 cm) pieces. Attach one 6mm jump ring to one side of the double-hole river rock. Attach one 5mm jump ring to the 6mm jump. Attach one 6mm jump ring to the 5mm jump ring, domed oval, and the end link of 1 piece of chain. Repeat this step to attach the other side of the river rock to the oval and second piece of chain.

4   Use one 5mm jump ring to attach the lobster clasp to the other end of 1 chain. Use one 6mm jump ring to attach the small river rock to the other end of the other piece of chain.

olive twist

Jane Dickerson

Try out this new polyester cable chain! The fabric texture looks great when paired with any kind of metal chain. The vintage brass chain shown is composed of elongated cable links and chain mail connectors. Mix shiny brass with tarnished, it looks great either way.

MATERIALS

12" (30.5 cm) of dark green polyester cable chain

9" (23 cm) of vintage brass 18×2mm elongated cable/chain mail chain

1 brass 50mm donut pendant

2 heavy brass 18mm rings

1 antique green copper 15mm jump ring

2 antique green copper 8mm jump rings

1 brass 11mm lobster clasp

TOOLS

2 pairs of chain-nose pliers

Heavy-duty scissors

Finished size: 17" (43 cm) with 2½" (6 cm) pendant drop

Resources: Polyester chain: Beadalon. Brass pendant and rings: Ashes to Beauty Adornments. Brass chain: Chelsea's Beads. Copper jump rings: Gems and Findings.

1 Cut the polyester chain into one 8" (20 cm) piece and one 4" (10 cm) piece. Open one 15mm jump ring and attach one end of the 8" (20 cm) piece of polyester chain and one end of the brass chain. Don't close the jump ring.

2 Thread the remaining 4" (10 cm) of polyester chain through the brass donut and bring both ends of the chain together. Thread both ends onto the 15mm jump ring, then close the jump ring.

3 Bring both ends of the necklace together and string on both brass rings. Push the rings down to the 15mm jump ring.

4 Attach one 8mm jump ring to the free end of the polyester chain. Use one 8mm jump ring to attach the lobster clasp to the free end of the brass chain.

color splash

Karen Keegan

Dress up any simple chain with loads of colorful dangles, creating a dramatic look with lots of movement. For a fuller look, add even more dangles!

MATERIALS

18" of sterling silver 10mm rolo chain

19 assorted 12mm lampworked glass saucer rondelles

18 assorted 11×5mm lampworked glass coins

13 assorted 4mm crystal cubes in coordinating colors

10 assorted 6mm crystal cubes in coordinating colors

38 sterling silver 2" head pins

1 silver S-hook clasp

TOOLS

Round-nose pliers

Chain-nose pliers

Wire cutters

Finished size: 18" (46 cm)

Beads and crystals: Supertime International. Chain, head pins, and clasp: Multi Creations, NJ.

1 Open one end of the hook clasp slightly and attach one end of the chain. Close that end of the hook. Use 1 head pin to string one 6mm cube and two 4mm cubes. Form a wrapped loop that attaches to the other end of the chain.

2 Use 1 head pin to string 1 coin. Form a wrapped loop that attaches to the center link of the chain.

3 Use 1 head pin to string 1 cube (either size) and 1 rondelle. Form a wrapped loop that attaches to the next chain link. Repeat entire step seventeen times, randomly stringing coins or cubes and rondelles.

4 Repeat Step 3 on the other side of the center link of chain. Hook the clasp on any link in the chain to shorten or lengthen, leaving the cubed dangle to hang down in the back for a nice finishing touch.

under lock and key

Melanie Brooks

Imagine an afternoon spent rummaging through treasure trunks of old skeleton keys, long forgotten padlocks, and bits of brass and rusty metal. This necklace is perfect for the treasure hunter in us all.

MATERIALS

12" (30.5 cm) of natural brass 4.5×6.2mm petite etched cable chain

1 desert pine 22mm square keyhole 3-strand porcelain pendant

1 desert pine 18mm square keyhole vertical porcelain link

2 desert pine 25×7mm screwed porcelain links

2 earth green 25×7mm screwed porcelain links

1 natural brass 11×20mm double-sided heart charm

2 natural brass 8×24mm key charms

4 natural brass 7×15mm fleur-de-lis charms

5 natural brass etched 9mm jump rings

11 natural brass 7mm jump rings (medium)

43 natural brass 5mm jump rings (small)

1 antique brass-plated 24mm lock-and-key toggle clasp

TOOLS

Round-nose pliers

2 pairs of chain-nose pliers

Flush cutters

Finished size: 22" (56 cm)

Porcelain: Melanie Brooks, Earthenwood Studio. Natural brass: Vintaj Natural Brass Co. Clasp: Ornamentea.

1 Use 1 small jump ring to attach the heart charm to the bottom loop on the small keyhole link. Use 2 small jump rings to attach 1 etched jump ring to the top of the link. Use 2 small jump rings to attach the etched jump ring to the bottom center loop of the large keystone pendant. Use round-nose pliers to form a loop at the top of 2 of the fleur-de-lis charms, but don't close the loops. Slide 1 fleur-de-lis charm into the bottom left loop on the pendant and close the loop to attach the charm. Repeat with the other charm, attaching it to the bottom right loop of the pendant.

2 Use 2 small jump rings to attach 1 etched jump ring to the top left loop of the large keystone pendant. Use 2 small jump rings to attach the same etched jump ring to the top center loop of the pendant. Use 2 small jump rings to attach 1 medium jump ring to the etched jump ring.

3 Cut a 5-link piece of chain. Open the last link in the chain and attach the medium jump ring from Step 2. Attach 1 small jump ring to 1 brass key charm. Use 1 medium jump ring to join the end link of the chain and the key charm. Use 2 small jump rings to attach the medium jump ring to a loop on 1 desert pine screwed link. Attach 2 small jump rings to the other loop of the desert pine screwed link. Attach 1 small jump ring to 1 fleur-de-lis charm. Cut a 5-link piece of chain. Use 1 medium jump ring to join the end link of the chain to the 2 small jump rings on the desert pine screwed link and the fleur-de-lis charm. Attach 1 medium jump ring to the other end of the chain. Use 2 small jump rings to attach the medium jump ring to a loop on 1 earthy green screwed link.

4 Use 2 small jump rings to attach the other loop on the earthy green screwed link to a medium jump ring. Cut a 4" (10 cm) piece of chain and open the last loop to attach to the medium jump ring. Use 1 small jump ring to attach the end of the chain to a large etched jump ring. Use 2 small jump rings to attach the large etched jump ring to 1 medium jump ring. Use 1 small jump ring to attach the medium jump ring to the key part of the clasp.

5 Repeat Steps 2 and 3, except begin by attaching the etched jump ring to the top right loop on the pendant. Use 2 small jump rings to attach the end loop of the earthy green screwed link to 1 medium jump ring. Cut a 4" (10 cm) piece of chain and open the last loop to attach to the medium jump ring. Use 1 small jump ring to attach the end of the chain to 1 etched jump ring. Use 1 small jump ring to attach the etched jump ring to the lock part of the clasp.

pocket watch

Jane Dickerson

When I saw these vintage watch faces, I pictured men's old-fashioned pocket watches dangling from vest pockets on beautiful gold chain. For an updated female version, I created a "pocket watch" lariat. The double-bar links in the chain are perfect for this design.

MATERIALS

26" (66 cm) of brass double-bar link chain

2 vintage 45mm watch faces

2 vintage 40mm watch faces

TOOLS

2 pairs of chain-nose pliers

Euro Tool 2-hole metal punch (¹⁄₁₆" and ³⁄₃₂")

2 brass 7×3mm micro screws and matching 4mm nuts

Ball-peen hammer

Flush cutters

Finished size: 29³⁄₈" (75 cm)

Watch faces: April Melody. Chain: The Bead Empire. Micro screws and nuts: Objects and Elements. Euro Tool 2-hole punch: Rings & Things.

1 The back of watch faces sometimes have pins sticking out. Cut the pins flush with flush cutters. Use the metal punch to drill a ¹⁄₁₆" (2 mm) hole in each watch face at 12:00, ⅛" (3.2 mm) from the edge. If necessary, drill a ¹⁄₁₆" (2 mm) hole in the center of each watch face.

2 Place the 45mm watch faces back to back. Remove 1 of the links from one end of the chain. Open the remaining link and thread it through both holes at 12:00; close the link. Repeat with the 40mm watch faces and the opposite end of the chain.

3 Thread 1 nut onto 1 screw and tighten it down to the head of the screw. Thread the screw through the center holes in the 45mm watch faces. Thread on 1 nut and screw it down until it is flush with the face. Use chain-nose pliers to tighten the nut. Trim the end of the screw with flush cutters to ⅛" (3.2 mm) above the nut. Using a ball-peen hammer, tap the end of the screw until it spreads out and flattens. Repeat with the 40mm watch faces.

sage offerings

Lorelei Eurto

This romantic necklace uses several different materials, blending ribbon, chain, ceramic, and brass into one harmonious whole. Tie a beautiful bow at the back of your neck and let the romance begin!

MATERIALS

5 sections, 6¾" (17 cm) each, of various size (2–8mm) brass cable chain

1 ceramic 26mm round pendant

1 brass 35mm blank round disc pendant

3 brass 10mm jump rings

6" (15 cm) of brass 24-gauge wire

24" (61 cm) of crinkly pale blue seam binding

TOOLS

2 pairs of chain-nose pliers

Wire cutters

Scissors

Finished size: 16–18" (41–46 cm)

Ceramic pendant: Chinook Jewelry. Brass blank disc pendant: Vintaj Natural Brass Co. Seam binding: Antica. Brass chain: AD Adornments, Vintaj Natural Brass Co., Fusion Beads, and Patina Queen. Brass wire: Patina Queen. Brass jump rings: Vintaj Natural Brass Co., Fusion Beads.

1 Use one 10mm jump ring to connect the ceramic pendant and the brass disc pendant.

2 Cut two 12" (30.5 cm) pieces of blue seam binding. Loop one end of 1 piece of seam binding through one 10mm jump ring. Use 3" (8 cm) of 24-gauge brass wire to tightly wrap the end of ribbon close to the ring several times tightly to secure. Trim any excess wire and binding. Repeat entire step for the second piece of seam binding using the third 10mm jump ring.

3 Open one 10mm jump ring with binding attached and attach it to one end of each of the 5 chains. Use all 5 chains to string the jump ring used in Step 1. Open the other 10mm jump ring with binding attached and attach it to the other ends of the 5 chains.

simplicity

Jane Dickerson

This simple little bracelet is beautiful and feminine. Using a rope chain to connect the bead links gives it just the right balance. It's lightweight and comfortable so you can wear it every day.

MATERIALS

7" (18 cm) of silver-plated 5×6mm flat wire oval link reverse rope chain

4 antique silver-plated 13×3mm flat oval ridged beads

6" (15 cm) sterling 16-gauge wire

1 sterling silver 5mm jump ring

1 sterling silver 13.2mm lobster clasp

TOOLS

Round-nose pliers

2 pairs of chain-nose pliers

Flush cutters

Finished size: 7" (18 cm)

Beads and chain: Chelsea's Beads.
Clasp and jump ring: Rio Grande.

1 Cut four ¾" (19 mm) pieces of chain. Cut four 1½" (4 cm) pieces of 16-gauge wire.

2 Use 1 wire to form a simple loop large enough for the lobster clasp to attach to. String 1 bead and form a simple loop that attaches to one end of 1 chain. Use 1 wire to form a simple loop that attaches to the other end of the chain. String 1 bead and form a simple loop that attaches to one end of another chain. Use 1 wire to form a simple loop that attaches to the other end of the chain. String 1 bead and form a simple loop that attaches to one end of another chain. Use 1 wire to form a simple loop that attaches to the other end of the chain. String 1 bead and form a simple loop that attaches to one end of the remaining chain.

3 Use the jump ring to attach the lobster clasp to the end of the last piece of chain added. Attach the clasp to the free simple loop on the first bead link.

connect five

Leslie Rogalski

Using figure-eight connectors at the center of this bracelet adds wonderful texture to the design. The angles of the curb chain contrasted with the smooth curves of the large rings all come together beautifully.

MATERIALS

6½" (16.5 cm) (14 links) of bright copper 12×9mm heavy curb chain

6" (15 cm) (27 links) of copper 8×6mm oval base metal cable chain

5 antique copper 16×3mm figure-eight connectors

5 copper 15mm jump rings

1 copper 18mm hook

TOOLS

2 pairs of chain-nose pliers

Flush cutters

Finished size: 7" (18 cm)

Connectors and jump rings: Gems and Findings. Curb chain: ABeadstore. Cable chain: Fusion Beads.

1   Cut two 13-link pieces of cable chain. Place the pieces of chain side by side. Attach 1 connector to the third link from the end of both chains. To close the connector, fold in the ends with chain-nose pliers, keeping the links of chain centered in each loop. Skip every other link and continue connecting the parallel links with 1 connector. The resulting chain will resemble a ladder with the connectors as the rungs.

2   Attach 2 jump rings to the last 2 chain links on each end of the cable chain. Make sure the chains are not twisted and the links are parallel. Do not close the jump rings yet.

3   Cut two 7-link pieces of curb chain. Take 1 piece of chain, bring the end links together, and thread both links onto both jump rings; close the jump rings. Attach the other piece of curb chain to the jump rings on the other end of the bracelet.

4   Open 1 jump ring and attach the fourth link of the curb chain; close the jump ring. Attach the hook clasp to the fourth link on the other end of the bracelet.

infinity

Taya and Silvija Koschnick

Four distinct chains are the focus of this delicate bracelet. Interlaced ovals in the center are counterbalanced by a small hand-drilled river rock.

MATERIALS

2¾" (7 cm) of sterling silver 1.5×2mm cable chain (small)

2¾" (7 cm) of sterling silver 2×3mm cable chain (medium)

2¾" (7 cm) of sterling silver 6×8mm flattened cable chain (large)

1¼" (3 cm) of sterling silver double-oval chain with 2 double ovals

1 small gray single-hole river rock

2 sterling silver 5mm jump rings

1 sterling silver 4mm jump ring

1 sterling silver 6mm jump ring

1 sterling silver 11mm lobster clasp

TOOLS

2 pairs of chain-nose pliers

Liver of sulfur

0000 extra-fine steel wool

Finished size: 7" (18 cm)

All materials: Bead Paradise.

1 Clean and oxidize all the sterling silver (see page 21 for instructions). Use the steel wool to gently remove the excess patina until you reach your desired shade.

2 Use one 5mm jump ring to attach one end of the double oval chain to one end of each of the small and medium cable chains. Use one 5mm jump ring to attach the other end of the double-oval chain to the large cable chain.

3 Use one 4mm jump ring to attach the lobster clasp to other ends of the small and medium cable chains. Use the 6mm jump ring to attach the river rock to the last link of the large cable chain.

splendid

Jane Dickerson

The pale blue and green raku beads by Keith O'Connor harmonize perfectly with the stoneware porcelain button by Lisa Peters. Mixing silver and gunmetal chain gives the piece both a matte and shiny finish. The button serves as a faux clasp because the necklace slips over your head!

MATERIALS

18" (46 cm) of silver 12×9mm cable chain

18" (46 cm) of gunmetal 6mm rolo chain

5 pale blue and green 14–16mm raku beads

1 pale blue/green 26mm stoneware porcelain button

2 sterling silver 8mm jump rings

10" (25 cm) sterling silver 14-gauge wire

TOOLS

2 pairs of chain-nose pliers

Round-nose pliers

Flush cutters

Finished size: 24" (61 cm)

Raku beads: Keith O'Connor. Stoneware porcelain button: Lisa Peters Art. Silver chain: The Bead Warehouse. Gunmetal chain: The Bead Empire. Silver wire: Metalliferous.

1 Cut six 3" (8 cm) pieces of silver chain and gunmetal chain. Cut five 2" (5 cm) lengths of wire.

2 Use 1 jump ring to attach one end each of 1 silver chain and 1 gunmetal chain to the button.

3 Use one length of wire and round-nose pliers to form a simple loop that attaches to the other end of the chains. String 1 raku bead and form a simple loop that attaches to one end each of 1 silver chain and 1 gunmetal chain.

4 Repeat Step 3 four times.

5 Use 1 jump ring to attach the other ends of the chains to the loop of the bottom and the first jump ring.

tinker toys

Jane Dickerson

These colorful tagua-nut discs are the perfect building blocks for a fast-and-fun necklace. You can keep it simple or embellish all the extra holes with drops and dangles and charms.

MATERIALS

3 red 8-hole 30mm roulettes

3 blue 8-hole 30mm roulettes

3 yellow 8-hole 30mm roulettes

3 green 8-hole 30mm roulettes

19 sterling silver 11.7mm soldered square rings

31 sterling silver 6mm jump rings

TOOLS

2 pairs of chain-nose pliers

Finished size: 24" (61 cm)

Tagua-nut roulettes: W. Bedoya Import Co.
Square rings and jump rings: Rio Grande.

1 Use 1 jump ring to attach 1 red roulette to 1 square ring.

2 Use 1 jump ring to attach the previous square ring to 1 blue roulette. Use 1 jump ring to attach the opposite hole of the blue roulette to 1 square ring.

3 Repeat Step 2 attaching 1 green roulette to the blue roulette and 1 yellow roulette to the green roulette.

4 Attach the remaining roulettes using the same technique and ending with 1 square ring.

5 Use 1 jump ring to attach 1 square ring to the previous square ring. Repeat six times, forming a chain of 8 square rings. Use 1 jump ring to attach the final square ring to the opposite hole of the first red roulette used.

bohemian heart

Lisa Blackwell

The eclectic mix of leather and chain gives this necklace an artsy, Bohemian feel. It's made of recycled materials and seems to have a story all its own.

9" (23 cm) (30 links) of brass
10mm round cable chain

1 decorated shibuichi 35×45mm
3-hole bohemian heart

1 shibuichi 25mm ring link

5 shibuichi 4×23mm plain
bone links

3 shibuichi 4×23mm
wire-wrapped bone links

9½" (24 cm) of brown 4mm
leather strip

9 brass 7mm jump rings

1 sterling silver 6mm
lobster clasp

10" (25 cm) of sterling silver
20-gauge wire

TOOLS

2 pairs of chain-nose pliers

Flush cutters

Scissors

E6000 glue

Finished size: 18¼" (46 cm)

*Bohemian heart, bone links, wire-wrapped
bone links, and ring link: Lisa and Tony
Blackwell, Zoa Art. Leather strips:
Marilyn Berg. Jump rings, lobster clasp,
and chain: Vintaj Natural Brass Co.*

1 Create a bone-link chain by connecting the links to-gether with jump rings in the following pattern: 3 plain bone links, 1 wire-wrapped bone link, 1 plain bone link, 2 wire-wrapped bone links, and 1 plain bone link. Use 1 jump ring to attach the end of the first link to the lob-ster clasp. Use 1 jump ring to attach the end of the last link to the side of the heart with 1 hole.

2 Remove an 8-link section from the brass chain. Attach one end to the bottom hole on the 2-hole side of the heart. Attach the other end to the 25mm ring. Remove a 20-link section from the remaining chain and attach one side to the 25mm ring. The catch on the lobster clasp will attach to the other end. Attach 1 link of the remaining chain (2 links) to the top hole of the heart.

3 Cut the leather into one 3½" (9 cm) piece and one 6" (15 cm) piece. Take the short piece of leather and fold ¾" (19 mm) around the last link of the 2-link chain from Step 2. Glue the fold to keep it in place. Fold ¾" (19 mm) of the other end around the ring link and glue that fold in place. Repeat with the 6" (15 cm) piece of leather, attaching one end to the ring link and the other end to the fifth link down from the free end of the chain.

4 Cut four 2½" (6 cm) pieces of wire. Wrap 1 piece of wire around each piece of leather at the glue point. Repeat for each glue point. Each wire wrap should sit next to the previous wrap. Trim the excess wire and use chain-nose pliers to tuck the end into the leather.

romance
Jane Dickerson

There is something very romantic about pearls. When matched with copper chain and glass, they are given a contemporary look, perfect for day or night.

MATERIALS

2¾" (7 cm) (4 links) of antique copper 30×9mm oval long-and-short chain

4½" (11 cm) (14 links) of antique copper 6×4mm oval long-and-short chain

3" (8 cm) (6 links) of antique copper 9mm round long-and-short copper chain

1 etched 48mm glass donut

30 round 6mm pearls

2 antique copper 4.5mm jump rings

1 antique copper 6mm jump ring

1 antique copper 8mm jump ring

8 copper 2mm crimp tubes

1 antique copper 18mm lobster clasp

16" of .015 flexible beading wire

TOOLS

2 pairs of chain-nose pliers

Crimping pliers

Wire cutters

Finished size: 17¼" (44 cm)

Pearls and glass donut: 1239 Broadway Corp. Round and oval chain: Rosalyn Designs. Small oval chain: Double Angel Designs. Copper jump rings and lobster clasp: The Bead Empire.

1   Remove a 2-link section from the large oval chain, leaving the middle connector in place. Separate the remaining links, leaving 1 connector attached to one end of each.

2   Pass the round chain through the donut and bring both ends together. Open the connector on 1 single large oval link and close it over both ends of the round chain. Repeat with the connector on the other large oval link.

3   Attach 4" (10 cm) of beading wire to the other end of 1 single oval link using 1 crimp tube. String 7 pearls, 1 crimp tube, and one end of the 2-link oval chain. Pass back through the tube and crimp.

4   Attach 4" (10 cm) of beading wire to the other end of the 2-link oval chain using 1 crimp tube. String 8 pearls, 1 crimp tube, and the 6mm jump ring. Pass back through the tube and crimp. Attach the 6mm jump ring to the lobster clasp.

5   Cut the small oval chain into two 7-link sections. Place the chain side by side and use one 4.5mm jump ring to connect the links on one end of each chain. Repeat for the other ends of the chain.

6   Attach 4" (10 cm) of beading wire to the other end of the remaining single oval link using 1 crimp tube. String 7 pearls, 1 crimp tube, and one 4.5mm jump ring. Pass back through the tube and crimp.

7   Attach 4" (10 cm) of beading wire to the 4.5mm jump ring on the end of the chains. String 8 pearls, 1 crimp tube, and the 8mm jump ring. Pass back through the tube and crimp.

gypsy delight

Jane Dickerson

Making a multistrand necklace can be a bit of a challenge, but take your time and enjoy the process. The chains used here are different sizes and textures, so you may need to make adjustments to the lengths depending upon the chain you use.

MATERIALS

6" (15 cm) of sterling silver 4mm rolo chain

8" (20 cm) of silver-plated 4×3mm oval chain

9½" (24 cm) of sterling silver 9mm round chain

10¾" (27 cm) of silver-plated 10mm coin chain

3 sterling silver 18-gauge 4mm jump rings

1 sterling silver 18-gauge 6mm jump ring

2 sterling silver 16-gauge 7mm jump rings

2 Nepalese silver 23×10mm end cones

1 sterling silver 13.2mm lobster clasp

4" (10 cm) of sterling silver 14-gauge wire

TOOLS

Round-nose pliers

2 pairs of chain-nose pliers

Wire cutters

Finished size: 16½" (42 cm)

Fine oval chain and coin chain: Chelsea's Beads. Round chain: Multi Creations, NJ. End cones: Bead Goes On. Rolo chain, lobster clasp, and jump rings: Rio Grande.

1 Remove the end connector links from the coin chain. Replace each connector link with one 4mm jump ring.

2 Attach one 7mm jump ring to one end of the coin necklace, one end of the round chain, and one end of the oval chain. Repeat for the other side of the necklace.

3 Use 2" (5 cm) of silver wire to form a simple loop that attaches to one 7mm jump ring used in Step 2. String 1 end cone and form a simple loop that attaches to 3" (8 cm) of rolo chain. Repeat for the other side of the necklace.

4 Use the 4mm jump ring to attach the lobster clasp to the other end of 1 of the rolo chains. Attach the 6mm jump ring to the other end of the other piece of rolo chain.

tweet

Lorelei Eurto

There are so many wonderful little flourishes in this necklace, from the filigree bead cap to the two jump rings capturing both strands of beads. And for a great finish, you can make your own clasp.

MATERIALS

6" (15 cm) of brass large loop chain

1 shell 25mm bird pendant

1 faceted 5×8mm Picasso Czech glass rondelle

2 bronze 4mm Czech glass cube beads

1 Canadian jade 10×15mm horse eye bead

300 matte green size 11° seed beads

1½" (4 cm) of brass 20-gauge wire

1 brass filigree bead cap

1 brass 10mm jump ring

9 brass 7mm jump rings

2 brass 2" (5 cm) eye pins

1 brass crimp bead

15" (38 cm) of .018 beading wire

TOOLS

2 pairs of chain-nose pliers

Round-nose pliers

Flat-nose pliers

Wire cutters

Finished size: 16¾" (43 cm)

Shell pendant: Lilly Pilly Designs. Chain: AD Adornments. Brass jump rings: Vintaj Natural Brass Co. Czech glass and seed beads: Emmi Beads. Jade: Lima Beads.

1 Attach one 7mm brass jump ring to the hole in the shell pendant. Attach the 10mm jump ring to the 7mm jump ring. Attach a chain of two 7mm jump rings to the 10mm jump ring.

2 Attach 1 eye pin to the previous 7mm jump ring. Use the eye pin to string 1 bronze glass cube, the faceted rondelle, and 1 bronze cube. Form a simple loop that attaches to one 7mm jump ring. Attach the jump ring to one end of 3" (8 cm) of chain.

3 Use the beading wire to string 300 seed beads. Pass the wire through the other end of the chain. Use both ends of the wire to string two 7mm jump rings. Use both ends of the wire to string 1 crimp bead and one 7mm jump ring. Bring both wires back through the crimp bead and crimp.

4 Attach the previous 7mm jump ring to one end of the remaining 3" (8 cm) of chain. Attach one 7mm jump ring to the other end of the chain. Use the remaining eye pin to string the bead cap and the jade bead. Form a wrapped loop that attaches to the previous 7mm jump ring. Attach one 7mm jump ring to the simple loop of the eye pin.

5 Make your own clasp: Form a simple loop on one end of the brass wire. Start curling the wire in a swirl shape using round-nose pliers. Place the swirl flat in the jaws of the flat-nose pliers, curving the wire around itself to make two large turns.

6 Attach the loop on the clasp to the last 7mm jump ring on the jade link. Hook the clasp into the 10mm jump ring to close the necklace.

eclectica

Jane Dickerson

Mixing bone, vintage Lucite, and several types of chain gives this piece a tribal feel with a modern twist. It's easy to make and fun to wear!

MATERIALS

7" (18 cm) of metal 18mm round cable chain

10" (25 cm) of metal 8×6mm oval cable chain

3½" (9 cm) of metal 15×10mm oval cable chain

2 rust-colored 20mm vintage Lucite discs

4 black-and-white 14mm bone discs

1 rust-and-brown 40×13mm vintage Lucite cylinder bead

1 white-and-black 40×9mm bone tube bead (large)

2 white-and-black 28×9mm bone tube beads (medium)

12" (30.5 cm) of sterling silver 14-gauge wire

1 sterling silver S-clasp

TOOLS

Round-nose pliers

2 pairs of chain-nose pliers

Wire cutters

Finished size: 26¼" (67 cm)

Small and large oval link chain: AD Adornments. Round chain: Michaels. Bone tube beads and bone disc beads: Ancient Moon Beads. Lucite beads: Chelsea's Beads. Silver wire: Metalliferous.

1 Cut the 8×6mm oval chain into two 4¾" (12 cm) (19-link) pieces. Cut the 15×10mm oval chain into two 1½" (4 cm) (3-link) pieces. Cut the round chain into one 4¼" (11 cm) (7-link) piece and one 1¼" (3 cm) (2-link) piece.

2 Attach one end of one 4¾" (12 cm) chain to one end of the clasp. Attach the other end of the chain to one end of one 1½" (4 cm) chain. Use 2¼" (6 cm) of wire to form a simple loop that attaches to the other end of the chain. Use the wire to string 1 bone disc and 1 Lucite disc twice. String 1 bone disc and form a simple loop that attaches to one end of the other 1½" (4 cm) chain.

3 Use 3" (8 cm) of wire to form a simple loop that attaches to the other end of the chain. String the large bone bead and form a simple loop that attaches to one end of the 4¼" (11 cm) chain. Use 2¾" (7 cm) of wire to form a simple loop that attaches to the other end of the chain. String the Lucite bead and form a simple loop that attaches to the 1¼" (3 cm) chain.

4 Use 3½" (9 cm) of wire to form a simple loop that attaches to the other end of the chain. String 1 medium bone bead, 1 bone disc, and 1 medium bone bead. Form a simple loop that attaches to one end of the remaining 4¾" (12 cm) chain.

copper sands

Jane Dickerson

Instead of a multistrand necklace with three different lengths, I've created this necklace so that each strand is almost the same length. When worn, all the strands come together for an easy, casual design.

1. Cut the 8×6mm chain into two 4" (10 cm) (17-link) pieces and four 1¼" (3 cm) (5-link) pieces. Cut the copper wire into five 4" (10 cm) pieces.

2. Use 1 wire to form a wrapped loop that attaches to one end of one 4" (10 cm) chain. String 1 bone disc and 1 horn disc twice. String 1 bone disc and form a wrapped loop that attaches to one end of one 1¼" (3 cm) chain.

3. Use 1 wire to form a wrapped loop that attaches to the other end of the previous chain. String 1 bone disc and 1 horn disc twice. String 1 bone disc and form a wrapped loop that attaches to one end of one 1¼" (3 cm) chain.

4. Repeat Step 3 three times, replacing the final 1¼" (3 cm) chain with the remaining 4" (10 cm) chain. Set aside.

5. Use the beading wire to string 1 crimp tube and 1 jump ring. Pass back through the tube and crimp. String 1 copper seed bead and 5 burgundy seed beads thirty-four times. String 1 copper seed bead, 1 crimp tube, and the other jump ring. Pass back through the tube and crimp.

6. Use 1 jump ring to attach one end of each size of chain to one half of the clasp. Repeat for the other end of the necklace.

MATERIALS

18½" (47 cm) of copper 12×8mm oval chain

14" (35.5 cm) of antique copper 8×6mm oval chain

10 burgundy 15mm horn disc beads

15 yellow 12mm bone disc beads

170 burgundy size 8° seed beads

35 matte copper size 6° seed beads

20" (50 cm) of copper 18-gauge wire

2 antique copper 8mm jump rings

2 copper 2mm crimp tubes

1 antique copper 12mm toggle clasp

23" (58 cm) of .015 flexible beading wire

TOOLS

Round-nose pliers

2 pairs of chain-nose pliers

Crimping pliers

Wire cutters

Finished size: 19¾" (50 cm)

Horn disc beads: Priscilla Beads and Jewelry. Bone disc beads: Kenneth Huang. Chain: 12×8mm oval chain: Rosalyn Designs; 8×6mm oval chain: Out on a Whim. Toggle clasp: Tierra Cast. Copper wire: Metalliferous. Copper seed beads: York Beads.

magic rings

Kerry Bogert

Enjoy the full, eye-catching colors in these disc beads by linking them together on their sides where you can see all the colorful layers and detail. Using short lengths of chain to connect each disc gives the piece movement and flexibility.

MATERIALS

30" (76 cm) of sterling silver 3.7mm flat cable chain

10 multicolored 11–13mm lampworked disc beads

8" (20 cm) each of 18-gauge colored copper wire in purple, red, and neon olivine

12" (30.5 cm) of 18-gauge colored copper wire in seafoam

1 sterling silver 16-gauge toggle bar

1 turquoise 6mm 16-gauge aluminum jump ring

TOOLS

Round-nose pliers

2 pairs of chain-nose pliers

Flush cutters

Finished size: 18" (46 cm)

Lampworked beads and toggle clasp: Kerry Bogert, Kab's Creative Concepts. Chain: Rio Grande. Colored copper wire: Parawire. Jump ring: Blue Buddha Boutique.

1 Cut the chain into ten 3" (8 cm) pieces.

2 Pass 1 chain through 2 glass discs. Cut 4" (10 cm) of colored copper wire and form a wrapped loop that attaches to the last link on one side of the chain. Begin a wrapped loop on the other end of the wire that attaches the other end of the chain. To complete this loop, wrap the wire over the previously wrapped wire, creating a double-wrapped loop.

3 Continue to build off this first link, adding one new disc each time with the same technique used in Step 2. The last disc is connected to the previous disc and unlinked on the opposite side. This disc will be the ring half of the clasp.

4 Pass the remaining 3" (8 cm) piece of chain through the first disc on your necklace. Use the 6mm jump ring to attach both ends of the chain to the bar half of the clasp.

city side

Lisa Blackwell

Inspired by city streets and alleyways, this bracelet is a mixture of recycled metals and vintage brass, giving it a unique, urban-chic look.

MATERIALS

2½" (6 cm) (7 links) of brass 10mm round cable chain

1 shibuichi 16×42mm oval bohemian focal piece

2 shibuichi 4×23mm plain bone links

1 shibuichi 4×23mm plain bone link with 6mm end ring

1 shibuichi 4×23mm plain double-bone link with 7mm oval end ring and 8mm floating ring

3 shibuichi 4×23mm wire-wrapped bone links

1 shibuichi 15mm disc

2 brass 7mm jump rings

5 brass 5×8mm oval jump rings

1 brass 13mm lobster clasp

TOOLS

2 pairs of chain-nose pliers

Finished size: 7¼" (18 cm)

Bohemian focal piece and bone links: Lisa and Tony Blackwell, Zoa Art. Chain, jump rings, and lobster clasp: Vintaj Natural Brass Co.

---

1 Use 1 oval jump ring to attach one side of the focal piece to one end of 1 wire-wrapped bone link. Use 1 oval jump ring to attach the other end of the wire-wrapped bone link to one end of 1 plain bone link. Continue attaching links with oval jump rings in the following order: 1 plain bone link and 2 wire-wrapped bone links.

2 Use 1 brass 7mm jump ring to attach the end of the last wire-wrapped bone link to the free end of the plain bone link with the 6mm ring on the other end. Use 1 brass 7mm jump ring to attach the previous 7mm jump ring to the lobster clasp. The lobster clasp attaches to the free side of the focal piece.

3 Remove a 3-link section of chain. Attach one end of the chain to the 6mm ring on the plain bone link and other end of the chain to the free end of the double-bone link (the one without the oval ring). Remove another 3-link section of chain and attach one end of the chain to the oval ring on the end of the double-bone link. Attach the other end of the chain to one side of the disc. Use the remaining link of chain to attach the other side of the disc to the focal piece.

best kept secret

Jane Dickerson

I love the look of chain mail, but I'm all fingers when it comes to connecting all those jump rings. So, look what I found! Shhhh, don't tell—it's chain mail chain! Simply attach a clasp and you'll look like you've spent hours creating this fast-and-easy bracelet.

MATERIALS

16" (40.5 cm) of antiqued brass 9mm chain mail chain

1 shibu 35mm Saki Silver toggle clasp

TOOLS

2 pairs of chain-nose pliers

Flush cutters

Finished size: 7½" (19 cm)

Chain mail chain: The Bead Empire.
Shibu toggle clasp (style: ss62): Saki Silver.

1 Cut the chain into two 6½" (16.5 cm) pieces and one 3" (7.5) piece. Place the 6½" (16.5 cm) pieces of chain side by side and disconnect 1 end link from each end of each piece of chain. You will be removing one 9mm jump ring and 2 twisted 6mm jump rings from each end.

2 Open 2 twisted 6mm jump rings from Step 1 and connect the end ring of the chain mail to one 9mm ring. Close the jump rings. Repeat with the 3 other ends of chain.

3 Remove two 9mm jump rings and 4 twisted 6mm jump rings from the scrap chain. Attach one 9mm jump ring to one half of the clasp. Repeat for the other half of the clasp.

4 Use 2 twisted 6mm jump rings from Step 3 to connect the 9mm jump ring on the toggle clasp and 1 end link of the bracelet. Connect the end link of the parallel chain to the toggle in the same way. Use 2 twisted 6mm jump rings to connect the 9mm jump ring on the ring side of the clasp with 1 end link on the bracelet. Repeat for the parallel link.

textures

Jane Dickerson

Using textured materials gives this fast-and-easy bracelet a weighty, substantial look, but it's really very light. With three simple ingredients, you can create a wonderful bracelet in minutes.

MATERIALS

7" (18 cm) of antique silver finish 15×11mm textured oval cable chain

4 antique silver finish 20mm textured washers

1 sterling silver 18.7mm lobster clasp

TOOLS

2 pairs of chain-nose pliers

Liver of sulfur

Pro polishing pad

Finished size: 7¾" (20 cm)

Chain and washers: AD Adornments.
Lobster clasp, liver of sulfur, and Pro
polishing pad: Rio Grande.

1 Oxidize the lobster clasp and remove any extra patina (see page 21 for instructions).

2 Separate the chain into three 3-link sections and two 2-link sections.

3 Attach one end of one 2-link section to 1 washer.

4 Attach one end of one 3-link section to the previous washer. Attach the other end of the chain to another washer.

5 Repeat Step 4 twice.

6 Attach one end of one 2-link section to the previous washer. Attach the other end of the chain to the lobster clasp.

be true

Lorelei Eurto

Mixed-media jewelry influenced this necklace that uses several types of metal and chain, glass, gemstones, pewter, and vintage glass. The colors for the beads were drawn from the beautiful etched lampworked glass lentil at the right side of the necklace.

MATERIALS

15½" (39 cm) of etched silver-plated 3mm cable chain

6½" (16.5 cm) of 6×15mm oxidized silver oval cable chain

1 brass 16mm oval chain link

1 lampworked 18×20mm lentil glass bead

1 lampworked 14mm glass ring

1 faceted 6×9mm rutilated quartz briolette

11 jade 3×5mm rondelles

1 flat 10×12mm oval rutilated quartz

3 cream Czech glass 6×20mm elongated bicones

1 brass 16×18mm bird connector

1 pewter 8×30mm feather charm

5 ornamental silver finish 5mm brass jump rings

3 silver finish 3mm brass jump rings

12 silver 2–3mm cornerless cubes

1 brass 4mm cube bead

2 silver 4mm heishi spacers

3" (7.5 cm) of silver 22-gauge artistic wire

6½" (16.5 cm) of .018 beading wire

11" (28 cm) of brass 24-gauge wire

4 brass crimp beads

1 sterling silver 9×22mm S-clasp with one 6mm soldered jump ring attached

TOOLS

Round-nose pliers

2 pairs of chain-nose pliers

Flush cutters

Crimping pliers

Finished size: 23" (58 cm)

Lampworked lentil bead: Kelley's Beads. Lampworked ring: Beads of Passion. Pewter charm: Green Girl Studios. Faceted briolette and Czech glass: Emmi Beads. Brass bird: Santa Barbara Designs. S-clasp, silver oval link chain, and Vintaj brass cube: Fusion Beads. Jump rings and etched silver-plated cable chain: AD Adornments. Brass wire: Patina Queen. Silver artistic wire and silver spacers: Michaels. Cornerless cubes: Elephant Eye Beads.

1 Use the 22-gauge wire to form a wrapped loop. String 1 cornerless cube, 1 heishi spacer, the glass lentil, 1 heishi spacer, and 1 cornerless cube. Form a wrapped loop. Set aside.

2 Attach one 5mm jump ring to the soldered ring on the S-clasp. Use one 3mm jump ring to attach the beak end of the bird connector to the 5mm jump ring. Use one 3mm jump ring to attach the tail end of the bird connector to one end of 8" (20 cm) of etched cable chain. Use one 5mm jump ring to attach the other end of the chain to the brass oval link.

3 Use 2½" (6 cm) of beading wire to string 1 crimp bead and the brass oval link. Pass back through the crimp bead and crimp. String 1 jade rondelle, 1 cornerless cube, 1 jade rondelle, 1 cornerless cube, the quartz oval, 1 cornerless cube, 1 jade rondelle, 1 cornerless cube, 1 jade rondelle, 1 crimp bead, and 1 of the wrapped loops from the link formed in Step 1. Pass back through the crimp bead and crimp.

4 Cut the remaining etched cable chain so that you have one 6" (15 cm) piece and one 1¼" (3.2 cm) piece. Use one 5mm jump ring to attach the 1¼" (3.2 cm) chain to the second wrapped loop of the link formed in Step 1. Use one 3mm jump ring to attach the leaf charm to the other end of the chain. Use 2" (5 cm) of brass wire and the rutilated quartz briolette to form a wrapped-loop briolette that attaches to the chain 1 link above the leaf charm.

5 Use one 5mm jump ring to attach one end of the 6" (15 cm) etched cable chain and one end of the oval cable chain to the second wrapped loop of the link formed in Step 1. Use one 5mm jump ring to attach the other ends of the chain to the glass ring.

6 Use 3" (7.5 cm) of brass wire to form a wrapped loop that attaches to the second 5mm jump ring used in Step 5. String 1 elongated bicone and form a wrapped loop. *Use 3" (7.5 cm) of brass wire to form a wrapped loop that attaches to the previous wrapped loop. String 1 elongated bicone and form a wrapped loop. Repeat from *. Use 4" (10 cm) of beading wire to string 1 crimp bead and the previous wrapped loop. Pass back through the crimp bead and crimp. String the brass cube and 1 jade rondelle. String 1 cornerless cube and 1 jade rondelle six times. String 1 crimp bead and the first 5mm jump ring used in Step 5. Pass back through the crimp bead and crimp.

beach memories

Lorelei Eurto

The pale matte green lampworked beads in this necklace remind me of beach glass; one of my favorite materials. The soothing palette in the choice of beads, contrasted with the shiny silver chain and focal pendant, create a fresh and beautiful design.

MATERIALS

10" (25 cm) of silver 5×9mm cable chain

2 etched green 8mm lampworked glass beads

4 faceted pale purple 3×5mm Czech glass rondelles

2 faceted green 5×8mm Czech glass rondelles

5 jade 14mm tube beads

3 gray 5mm Job's Tears seeds

1 pewter 7mm pod charm

1 silver 25mm ring

2 silver 7mm Karen hill tribe spacers

6 silver-toned 4mm rondelles

1 silver 3mm jump ring

26" (66 cm) of silver 24-gauge artistic wire

1 silver lobster clasp

TOOLS

Round-nose pliers

2 pairs of chain-nose pliers

Flush cutters

Finished size: 20¾" (53 cm)

Pewter pod charm: Mamacita Beadworks. Silver ring: Wynwood's. Lampworked glass: Cindy Hoo. Jade tubes: Emmi Beads. Job's Tears seeds: The Saffron House. Silver spacers and lobster clasp: Fusion Beads. Silver-tone rondelles and chain: Michaels. Czech glass: Beadaliferous.

1 Cut 6" (15 cm) of cable chain. Use 2" (5 cm) of 24-gauge wire to form a wrapped loop that attaches to one end of the chain. String 1 Job's Tear seed and form a wrapped loop.

2 Use 2" (5 cm) of wire to form a wrapped loop that attaches to the previous wrapped loop. String 1 green rondelle and form a wrapped loop. Repeat using 1 jade tube. Repeat using 1 Job's Tear seed. Repeat using 3" (7.5 cm) of wire and stringing 1 jade tube, 1 silver-toned rondelle, and 1 jade tube. Repeat using 2" (5 cm) of wire and stringing 1 purple rondelle, 1 silver spacer, and 1 purple rondelle. Repeat, stringing 1 silver-toned rondelle, 1 lampworked glass bead, and 1 silver-toned rondelle and attaching the final wrapped loop to one end of 1" (2.5 cm) of chain.

3 Open the other end of the 1" (2.5 cm) chain and attach it to the pewter pod charm and the silver ring. Repeat using one end of the remaining 3" (7.5 cm) of chain. Use 2" (5 cm) of wire to form a wrapped loop that attaches to the other end of the chain. String 1 green rondelle and form a wrapped loop.

4 Use 2" (5 cm) of wire to form a wrapped loop that attaches to the previous wrapped loop. String 1 purple rondelle, 1 silver spacer, and 1 purple rondelle and form a wrapped loop. Repeat using 3" (7.5 cm) of wire and stringing 1 jade tube, 1 silver-toned rondelle, and 1 jade tube. Repeat using 2" (5 cm) of wire and stringing 1 Job's Tear seed. Repeat stringing 1 silver-toned rondelle, 1 lampworked glass bead, and 1 silver-toned rondelle.

5 Use the jump ring to attach the lobster clasp to the previous wrapped loop.

quick links

Jane Dickerson

This fast-and-easy necklace uses hardware store rubber O-rings to create a fun necklace with a bit of an edge. You can try it using heavier chain, too, and you'll have a totally different look.

MATERIALS

14" (35.5 cm) of red enamel 5.5×4mm oval cable chain

14" (35.5 cm) of black 10×8mm oval cable chain

2 (small) O-rings: $^{13}/_{16}$ ID, $^{1}/_{16}$ OD

2 (medium) O-rings: $^{7}/_{8}$ ID, $^{1}/_{8}$ OD

1 (large) O-ring: $^{5}/_{16}$ ID, $^{9}/_{16}$ OD

11 sterling silver 8mm jump rings

1 sterling silver 10mm jump ring

1 sterling silver 18.7mm lobster clasp

TOOLS

2 pairs of chain-nose pliers

Wire cutters

Finished size: 20½" (52 cm)

Rubber O-rings from Storehouse Kit: Harbor Freight. Lobster clasp and jump rings: Rio Grande. Black chain: AD Adornments. Red enamel chain: MyElements.

1   Oxidize the jump rings and lobster clasp. See page 21 for instructions on oxidizing.

2   Cut four 3⅜" (9 cm) (25-link) pieces of red enamel chain. Cut four 3¼" (8 cm) (11-link) pieces of black chain.

3   Use one 8mm jump ring to attach the 10mm jump ring to 1 small O-ring.

4   Use one 8mm jump ring to attach the O-ring from the previous step to one end each of 1 red and 1 black chain.

5   Use one 8mm jump ring to attach the other ends of the chains to 1 medium O-ring. Repeat Step 4.

6   Use one 8mm jump ring to attach the other ends of the chains to the large O-ring. Repeat Step 4. Repeat Step 5.

7   Use one 8mm jump ring to attach the other ends of the chains to 1 small O-ring. Use one 8mm jump ring to attach the O-ring to another 8mm jump ring and the lobster clasp.

klimt delight

Lorelei Eurto

Inspired by the art of Gustav Klimt, the colors of the focal bead set the tone for this delightful asymmetrical necklace. It can be worn several different ways with either the chain or the triple-strand section as the focal point of this necklace. The porcelain focal bead can sit at the side or at the front.

MATERIALS

8½" (22 cm) of copper fringe chain

8" (20 cm) of brass 4mm cable chain

1 cylinder 15×24mm porcelain focal bead

6 etched rust 5×8mm lampworked glass beads

1 etched black 5×8mm lampworked glass bead

8 bronze 4mm Czech glass rondelles

8 jade 3×5mm rondelles

101 copper size 11° seed beads

4 bronze size 8° glass seed beads

2 brass 4mm corrugated round beads

2 copper 8mm bead caps

1 brass hammered ring

1 brass filigree tube bead

5½" (14 cm) of brass 20-gauge wire

24" (61 cm) of brass 24-gauge wire

9" (23 cm) of .018 beading wire

1 brass 2" (5 cm) eye pin

2 brass 6mm jump rings

3 brass 4mm jump rings

2 brass crimp beads

TOOLS

Round-nose pliers

2 pairs of chain-nose pliers

Flush cutters

Crimping pliers

Finished size: 20½" (52 cm)

Porcelain barrel focal bead: Lumina. Copper bead caps: Lisa Ortisan. Fringe chain: AD Adornments. Lampworked glass: Cindy Hoo. Jade rondelles: Yadana Beads. Vintaj brass: Fusion Beads. Glass seed beads and rondelles: Emmi Beads. Brass wire: Patina Queen.

1 Attach one 6mm jump ring to the hole on the hammered brass ring. Cut 2½" (6 cm) of 20-gauge brass wire. Form a wrapped loop that attaches to the jump ring on the hammered ring. String 1 rust bead, 1 jade rondelle, and 1 rust bead. Form a wrapped loop that attaches to one end of the fringe chain.

2 Cut 3" (8 cm) of 20-gauge wire and form a wrapped loop that attaches to the other end of the fringe chain. String 1 copper bead cap, the porcelain focal bead, and 1 copper bead cap. Form a wrapped loop that attaches to one end of the cable chain.

3 Use the beading wire to string 1 crimp bead and the previous wrapped loop. Pass back through the crimp bead and crimp. String 87 copper seed beads, 1 crimp bead, and one 6mm jump ring. Pass back through the crimp bead and crimp. Attach the 6mm jump ring to the free end of the cable chain.

4 Use 2" (5 cm) of 24-gauge wire to form a wrapped loop that attaches to the second wrapped loop formed in Step 2. String 1 bronze rondelle, 1 rust bead, and 1 bronze rondelle. Form a wrapped loop.

5 Use 2" (5 cm) of 24-gauge wire to form a wrapped loop that attaches to the previous wrapped loop. String 1 copper seed bead, 1 jade rondelle, and 1 copper seed bead. Form a wrapped loop.

6 Repeat Step 5.

7 Use 2" (5 cm) of 24-gauge wire to form a wrapped loop that attaches to the previous wrapped loop. String 1 bronze rondelle, 1 rust bead, and 1 bronze rondelle. Form a wrapped loop.

8 Repeat Step 5. Repeat Step 7. Repeat Step 5 twice. Repeat Step 7.

9 Use 2" (5 cm) of 24-gauge wire to form a wrapped loop that attaches to the previous wrapped loop. String 1 copper seed bead, the black lampworked glass bead, and 1 copper seed bead. Form a wrapped loop.

10 Repeat Step 5. Repeat Step 5 again, attaching the final wrapped loop to the 6mm jump ring from Step 3.

11 Use the eye pin to string 1 brass corrugated bead, 1 bronze seed bead, 1 brass filigree tube bead, 1 bronze seed bead, and 1 brass corrugated bead, and form a simple loop. Open one 4mm jump ring and thread it into and out of 2 centrally located holes in the side of the filigree tube bead. Close the jump ring. Connect a chain of 2 more 4mm jump rings to the 4mm jump ring. Attach the third jump ring in the chain to the 6mm jump ring from Step 3.

think of me

Lorelei Eurto

When you wear this lovely bracelet, you'll be reminded of your special someone every time you glance at the beautiful pewter heart charm.

MATERIALS

6¾" (17 cm) of brass cable chain

5 freshwater pearls in various warm tones

96 iridescent pink size 11° seed beads

1 bronze 5mm Czech glass bead

2 gray 12mm mother-of-pearl coins

1 white 13mm freshwater pearl coin

1 pewter heart charm

14" (35.5 cm) of brass 24-gauge wire

9" (23 cm) of .018 beading wire

6" (15 cm) of blue seam binding

6" (15 cm) of brown seam binding

2 brass crimp beads

2 brass 5mm jump rings

1 brass swirl hook clasp

TOOLS

Round-nose pliers

2 pairs of chain-nose pliers

Crimping pliers

Wire cutters

Scissors

Finished size: 7½" (19 cm)

Pewter heart charm: Green Girl Studios. Silk seam binding: Antica. Brass chain: AD Adornments. Brass wire: Patina Queen. Beading wire, seed beads, crimps, mother-of-pearl beads, pearls, and Czech glass: Emmi Beads. Handmade designer clasp: Lorelei Eurto.

1 Open the last link on one end of the brass chain and attach the charm; close the link.

2 Attach one end of the beading wire to one 5mm jump ring using 1 crimp bead. String 96 seed beads, 1 crimp bead, and one 5mm jump ring. Pass back through the crimp bead and crimp. Attach one of the jump rings to the link of chain with the charm. Attach the other jump ring to the second-to-last link of the other end of the chain.

3 Cut 1½" (4 cm) of 24-gauge brass wire and form a wrapped loop. String 1 purple pearl and form a wrapped loop that attaches to the link of chain with the charm.

4 Use 1½" (4 cm) of wire to form a wrapped loop that attaches to the previous empty wrapped loop. String 1 pearl and form a wrapped loop. Repeat entire step seven times, adding beads in this order: white pearl coin, mother-of-pearl coin, pearl, bronze glass bead, pearl, mother-of-pearl coin, and pearl, and attaching the final wrapped loop to the second-to-last link of the other end of the chain.

5 Cut 3 pieces of blue seam binding and 3 pieces of brown seam binding, each 2" (5 cm) long. Alternating colors, tie and knot the seam binding onto the chain links so that there are 3 links of chain between each piece.

6 Attach the clasp to the chain link with the charm. The hook will attach to the end link on the opposite side of the bracelet.

urban cluster

Lisa Blackwell

The materials in this necklace are a cluster of recycled metals, vintage brass, and leather. Inspired by the city, it holds tales of urban life renewed.

MATERIALS

6½" (16.5 cm) (21 links) of brass 10mm round cable chain

9¼" (24 cm) of brass 6mm oval cable chain

2 bronze 4–5mm freshwater pearls

1 shibuichi 23mm ring link

10" (25 cm) strip of gold 5mm leather

2 shibuichi charms

1 resin leaf head pin

1 sterling silver 20-gauge head pin

10" (25 cm) of sterling silver 20-gauge wire

1 brass 6mm lobster clasp

TOOLS

Round-nose pliers

2 pairs of chain-nose pliers

Flush cutters

Scissors

E6000 glue

Finished size: 20" (51 cm)

Ring link, charms, and resin leaf head pin: Lisa and Tony Blackwell, Zoa Art. Chain and lobster clasp: Vintaj Natural Brass Co. Leather: Marilyn Berg.

1 Begin a wrapped loop about ¼" (6.4 mm) above the top of the leaf on the resin leaf head pin. Before completing the wrap, attach the head pin to 1 hole of the ring link. This will be the "bottom" of the ring.

2 Remove 1 link from the round cable chain and attach both charms to the ring link. Use the head pin to string the 2 pearls and form a wrapped loop that attaches to the bottom hole of one of the charms.

3 Attach the end link on the oval chain to 1 of the top holes on the ring link. Attach the other end of the chain to the loop on the lobster clasp.

4 Cut the leather into four 2½" (6 cm) strips. Take 1 piece of leather and fold one end to the middle of the strip, then fold the other end so it overlaps the first end in the middle. Glue the leather in place where it overlaps. Repeat two times. Pass the remaining leather through the ring link. Fold and glue the leather in the middle as before.

5 Cut four 2½" (6 cm) pieces of wire. Wrap 1 piece of wire around each piece of leather at the glued joint. Each wrap should sit next to the previous wrap, covering the join completely. Trim the excess wire and tuck in the end with chain-nose pliers.

6 Cut the round chain into four 5-link pieces. Open the end link on one 5-link piece of chain. Pass the link through the fold in the leather strip, starting with the end fold of the leather strip attached to the ring link. Continue connecting the leather strips together with 5-link sections, ending with a 5-link piece of chain.

queen for a day
Lorelei Eurto

If the crown fits, wear it! This funky and modern bracelet has just the right charm, and now you can be Queen for a day or more.

MATERIALS

6" (16 cm) of brass 6.5×9.5mm etched cable chain

1 carved 10mm bone bead

1 twisted 8×15mm ebony wood barrel bead

1 cream-and-black 12mm etched lampworked glass bead

1 burgundy 10mm etched lampworked glass bead

1 cream 5×10mm etched lampworked glass bead

1 bronze 2mm Czech glass cube bead

1 wood 15mm disc bead with image of crown

1 brass 2" (5 cm) head pin

10" (25 cm) of 20-gauge brass wire

3" (8 cm) of 20-gauge brass wire for clasp

TOOLS

Round-nose pliers

2 pairs of chain-nose pliers

Wire cutters

Finished size: 7½" (19 cm)

Lampworked glass: Cindy Hoo. Wood: E&E Bungalow. Carved bone: Emmi Beads. Chain: Vintaj Natural Brass Co. Brass wire: Patina Queen. Queen bead: Beady Monkey.

1 To create the hook style clasp, make a wrapped loop at one end of the 3" (8 cm) piece of brass wire. Curve the straight portion of the wire around the large end of the round-nose pliers, about ¾" (19 mm) from the wrapped loop. Curl the tip of the wire up using chain-nose pliers.

2 Use 2" (5 cm) of brass wire to form a wrapped loop that attaches to the hook clasp. String the cream 5x10mm lampworked glass bead and form a wrapped loop. Use 2" (5 cm) of wire to form a wrapped loop that attaches to the previous wrapped loop. String the wood barrel bead and form a wrapped loop that attaches to both ends of a 4½" (12 cm) piece of chain.

3 Use 2" (5 cm) of wire to form a wrapped loop that attaches to the middle link of the chain. String the burgundy lampworked glass bead and form a wrapped loop. Use 2" (5 cm) of wire to form a wrapped loop that attaches to the previous wrapped loop. String the cream 12mm lampworked glass bead and form a wrapped loop. Use 2" (5 cm) of wire to form a wrapped loop that attaches to the previous wrapped loop. String the carved bone bead and form a wrapped loop that attaches to one end of the remaining piece of chain.

4 Use the head pin to string the crown bead and the bronze cube. Form a wrapped loop that attaches to the other end of the chain.

Contributors

Lisa Blackwell and her husband, Tony, have combined their artistic talents into a business, Zoa Art. Tony does the glasswork and casting, while Lisa works with PMC, silver designs, and completed jewelry. Their newer work includes shibuichi, a copper/silver alloy, and thoughts of other metals are blooming. You can see more of their work at zoaart.com and zoaart.etsy.com.

Kerry Bogert is the lampworked-glass artist and wire jewelry designer behind Kab's Concepts. She has been working with glass and wire for more than five years and is currently working with Interweave on her first book, which will be published in Spring 2010. To find out more about her work, visit kabsconcepts.com or contact her at kerry@kabsconcepts.com.

Melanie Brooks has been hand-crafting porcelain beads, charms, and components with her business Earthenwood Studio for over ten years. She sells her detailed ceramic works through her website EarthenwoodStudio.com.

Jane Dickerson is managing editor of *Step by Step Beads*, editor of *Creative Jewelry*, contributing editor to *Step by Step Wire Jewelry*, and project manager for the first series of *Bead Fest Video Workshops*. Her work has appeared in *Step by Step Beads*, *Creative Jewelry*, and *Easy Wire* magazines, and *101 Wire Earrings* (Interweave).

Lorelei Eurto is a self-taught jewelry designer. She lives in upstate New York with her husband and spoiled cat, Marley. Lorelei works full-time as an assistant registrar at a local art museum, and designs jewelry part-time in the evenings and mostly on weekends. She has been selling her designs in the museum's gift shop and on Etsy for about two years. You can see more of her jewelry at Lorelei1141.etsy.com and 1000markets.com/users/theowlsden. Read more about her process on her blog, http://Lorelei1141.blogspot.com.

Yvonne Irvin has been creating one-of-a-kind objects of art since her early childhood. Most recently, Yvonne was invited by the Philadelphia Museum of Art to display and sell her finished jewelry at their exclusive Artworks Gallery. Yvonne sells her proprietary MyELEMENTS components at select bead shops, shows, and myelements.etsy.com. Kits and finished jewelry are available on her website. Yvonne can be reached at info@myelementsbyyvonne.com.

Karen Keegan has been making custom jewelry creations for five years through her business, Karen Keegan Designs, and has been a decorative painter for over fifteen years. Currently, she is the event manager for Bead Fest.

Taya and Silvija Koschnick grew up making jewelry with their mother, a jeweler and longtime bead-store owner. Together, the two sisters started Tasi Designs, tasidesigns.etsy.com, a unique jewelry line that blends precious metals, natural stones, and historically rich antique and ancient trade beads.

Denise Peck is editor in chief of *Step by Step Wire Jewelry* and senior editor of *Jewelry Artist*. An editor by trade and a lifelong lover of jewelry, she was able to pursue both when she joined *Lapidary Journal* in 2004. She has a bench jeweler's certificate from Studio Jeweler's Ltd. Denise has published two books with Interweave: *Wire Style* and *101 Wire Earrings*.

Leslie Rogalski is editor in chief of *Step by Step Beads* and *Creative Jewelry*, and is a contributing editor to *Step by Step Wire Jewelry*. A frequent presenter on the PBS TV show *Beads, Baubles & Jewels*, she has been an artist and writer (among other things) all her life.

Resources

1239 Broadway Corp.
1239 Broadway 2nd Fl.
New York, NY 10001
(800) 275-7967
1239corp.com

ABeadstore
(800) 532-8480
abeadstore.com

AD Adornments
2464 West Estes, Unit 1
Chicago, IL 60645
(773) 338-3818
adadornments.com

Ancient Moon Beads
409 Mt. Auburn St.
Watertown, MA 02472
(617) 926-1887
ancientmoon.com

Antica
antica.etsy.com

April Melody
aprilmelody.com

Ashes to Beauty Adornments
115 Camino de las Huertas
Placitas, NM 87043
(505) 867-4244
Ashes2Beauty.com

The Bead Empire
1032 Avenue of the Americas #3
New York, NY 10018
(212) 768-8818

The Bead Goes On
2700 Avenger Dr., Ste. 111
Virginia Beach, VA 23452
(866) 861-2323
beadgoeson.com

Bead Paradise
29 West College St.
Oberlin, OH 44074
(440) 775-2233
beadparadise.com

The Bead Warehouse
2740 Garfield Ave.
Silver Spring, MD 20910
(301) 565-0487
thebeadwarehouse.com

Beadalon
440 Highlands Blvd.
Coatesville, PA 19320
(866) 423-2325
www.beadalon.com

Beads of Passion
beadsofpassion.etsy.com

Beady Monkey
beadymonkey.etsy.com

Blue Buddha Boutique
4533 N. Kedzie
Chicago, IL 60625
(866) 602-7464
bluebuddhaboutique.com

Braker Beads
16813 Mansion Rd.
New Berlin, IL 62670
BrakerBeads.com

Chelsea's Beads
1799 St. Johns Ave.
Highland Park, IL 60035
(847) 433-3451
chelseasbeads.com

Chinook Jewelry
PO Box 420232
San Diego, CA 92142
chinookjewelry.com

Cindy Hoo
cindyhoo.etsy.com

Deepwood Art
Fran Lizardi
DeepwoodArt.com

Distracted Muse
Stefanie Meisel
distractedmuse.etsy.com

Double Angel Designs
doubleangeldesign.etsy.com

E&E Bungalow
eandebungalow.etsy.com

Earthenwood Studio
Melanie Brooks
PO Box 20002
Ferndale, MI 48220
(248) 548-4793
EarthenwoodStudio.com

Elephant Eye Beads
PO Box 41
Pollocksville, NC 28573
(252) 229-1040
elephanteyebeads.com

EmMi Beads
3 Fountain St., Ste. 202
Clinton, NY 13323
(315) 853-8760
emmibeads.com

ExpeditionD
ExpeditionD.etsy.com

Fire Mountain Gems and Beads
One Fire Mountain Wy.
Grants Pass, OR 97526
(800) 355-2137
firemountaingems.com

Fusion Beads
13024 Stone Ave. N.
Seattle, WA 98133
(888)781-3559
fusionbeads.com

Gaea
PO Box 684
Ojai, CA 93023
(805) 640-8989
gaea.cc

Gems and Findings
gemsandfindings.com

Green Girl Studios
PO Box 19389
Asheville, NC 28815
(828) 298-2263
greengirlstudios.com

Guy Melamed
guymelamed.etsy.com

Hands of the Hills
3016 78th Ave. SE
Mercer Island, WA 98040
(206) 232-4588
hohbead.com

Harbor Freight
harborfreight.com

Hip Chicks Beads
4414 160th Cir.
Urbandale, IA 50323
(515) 771-8600
HipChickBeads.com

Hobby Lobby
hobbylobby.com

Home Depot
homedepot.com

Hour Glass Productions
hourglassproductions.etsy.com

Humblebeads
humblebeads.etsy.com

Jewelry Supply
(866) 380-7464
jewelrysupply.com

JoAnne Zekowski
zdesigns@mindspring.com

Jubilee
jubilee.etsy.com

Kab's Creative Concepts
Kerry Bogert
5799 Coppersmith Tr.
Ontario, NY 14519
(585) 944-0141
kabsconcepts.com

Keith O'Connor
(603) 772-4269
kbocraku@aol.com

Kelley's Beads
kelleysbeads.etsy.com

Kenneth Huang
40 E. 78th St. #10A
New York, NY 10001
(212) 988-7333

Keoki Art Glass
KeokiArtGlass@hotmail.com

Laura Drosner Schreiber
LampworkbyLaura.com

Lilly Pilly Designs
PO Box 270136
Louisville, CO 80027
(303) 543-8673
lillypillydesigns.com

Lima Beads
(888) 211-7919
limabeads.com

Lisa Ortisan
kissingdogdesigns.etsy.com

Lisa Peters Art
(201) 784-0812
lisapetersart.com

Lorelei Eurto
lorelei1141.etsy.com

Lumina
PO Box 190722
Dallas, TX 75219
(800) 737-0668
2candc.com

Mamacita Beadworks
mamacitabeadworks.etsy.com

Marilyn Berg
2405 1st Ave.
Seattle, WA
(206) 448-2480
marilynberg.com

Metalliferous
34 W. 46th St.
New York, NY 10036
(212) 944-0909
metalliferous.com

Michaels
michaels.com

Multi Creations Inc.
(732) 607-6422
multicreationsnj.com

MyElements
Yvonne Irvin
myelements.etsy.com

Nina Designs
PO Box 8127
Emeryville, CA 94662
(800) 336-6462
ninadesigns.com

Objects and Elements
23216 E. Echo Lake Rd.
Snohomish, WA 98296
(206) 965-0373
objectsandelements.com

Ornamentea
509 N. West St.
Raleigh, NC 27603
(919) 834-6260
ornamentea.com

Out on a Whim
121 E. Cotati Ave.
Cotati, CA 94931
(800) 232-3111
whimbeads.com

Parawire
2-8 Central Ave.
East Orange, NJ 07018
(973) 672-0500
parawire.com

Patina Queen
patinaqueen.etsy.com

Priscilla Beads and Jewelry
325 Pershing Ave.
Carteret, NJ 07008
(732) 322-3488
priscillabeadsandjewelry.com

Rings & Things
PO Box 450
Spokane, WA 99210
(800) 366-2156
rings-things.com

Rio Grande
7500 Bluewater Rd. NW
Albuquerque, NM 87121
(800) 545-6566
riogrande.com

Riverstone Bead Company
6131 Hemlock Ave.
Miller Beach, IN 46403
(219) 939-2050
riverstonebead.com

Rosalyn Designs
rosalyndesigns.etsy.com

The Saffron House
saffronhouse.etsy.com

Saki Silver
625 Eveningstar Ln.
Cincinnati, OH 45990
(513) 221-5480
sakisilver.com

Santa Barbara Designs
santabarbaradesigns.etsy.com

Silk Road Treasures
28401 Ballard Dr., Unit F
Lake Forest, IL 60045
(847) 918-1066
silkroadtreasures.com

Some Enchanted Beading
someenchantedbeading@
yahoo.com
someenchantedbeading.com

Sunyno
sunyno.etsy.com

Supertime International
8687 Grovemont Cir.
Gaithersburg, MD 20877
(800) 878-2943
supertimebeads.com

Terrestrial
terrestrial.etsy.com

Tierra Cast
3177 Guerneville Rd.
Santa Rosa, CA 95401
(800) 222-9939
tierracast.com

Vintaj Natural Brass Co.
PO Box 246
Galena, IL 61036
vintaj.com

W. Bedoya Import Co.
56-01 Nurge Ave.
Maspeth, NY 11378
(718) 366-1190
bedexport.com

The Wishing Bead
thewishingbead.etsy.com

Wynwood's
940 Water St.
Port Townsend, WA 98368
(888) 311-6131
wynwoods.com

Yadana Beads
yadanabeads.etsy.com

York Beads
10 W. 37th St.
New York, NY 10018
(800) 223-6676
yorkbeads.com

Zippybeads
zippybeads.etsy.com

Zoa Art
Lisa and Tony Blackwell
zoaart.com

Index

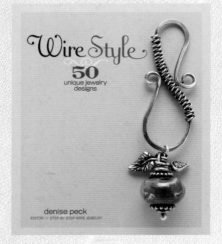
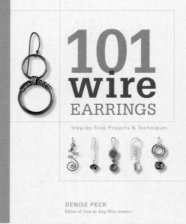
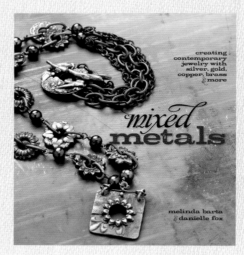